Legalised Leadership

The Bedford Way Papers Series

Legalised Leadership
Law-based educational reform in England and its effect on headteachers

Dan Gibton

Bedford Way Papers

INSTITUTE OF
EDUCATION
UNIVERSITY OF LONDON

First published in 2004 by the Institute of Education, University of London,
20 Bedford Way, London WC1H 0AL
www.ioe.ac.uk

© Institute of Education, University of London 2004

Over 100 years of excellence in education

British Library Cataloguing in Publication Data:
A catalogue record for this publication is available from the British Library

ISBN 0 85473 701 4

Dan Gibton asserts the moral right to be identified as the author of this work.

Text design by Joan Rose
Cover design by Andrew Chapman
Page make-up by Cambridge Photosetting Services, Cambridge

Production services by
Book Production Consultants plc, Cambridge

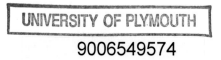

To my dear parents, Joab and Dinah, for their help and support, with endless love.

Contents

Figures and tables

Figures

Tables

Foreword

I am delighted to be able to contribute a foreword to this important book. In *Legalised Leadership* Dan Gibton attempts, successfully, to examine how law-based reform has impacted upon schools in England and more particularly on the practices of headteachers. As an Israeli he refers to himself as a 'foreigner doing research in a foreign land' and asks whether it is fruitful or detrimental to his research. He has nothing to worry about and his experience and knowledge of several other education systems brings a strength to the research and results in a broad and objective view.

The research upon which this book is based is described as a qualitative multiple case study. Data were gathered from 29 schools of mixed types, including grammar and specialist schools and those involved in Education Action Zones. The lengthy interviews with headteachers of these schools were supplemented by data derived from a small-scale national survey of heads. Through these methods Gibton attempts to understand how education policy is seen through the eyes of the main players – principals/headteachers – arguing that this can provide insights into how policy is implemented and why it succeeds or fails. His interest is in identifying the socio-political forces that are behind such policies and how they are implemented.

The central focus of the book is law-based reform and educational leadership. The former refers to the widespread reform agenda brought about by legislation, such as the move to decentralise and give schools greater autonomy whilst retaining control, especially over the curriculum, and 'steering at a distance' from the centre. What is exceptional about this study and which sets it apart from an ever-burgeoning literature on educational leadership, is that it has important things to say about educational law and how this has impacted upon school leadership, especially headship. Gibton's main thesis is that law-based reform in England disregards the circumstances of educational leadership. It is headteachers who are the main conduits through which law-based reform attempts to achieve its goals within educational policy. The author documents the severe pressures on heads which these reforms often bring about but which are unnecessary and irrelevant to the reforms' objectives. The study is also about (new) Labour government's attempt to reshape the school system and how heads views this. Most are supportive of its initial intentions but disappointed by what has not been achieved.

The study is exceptional in other ways too. It is scholarly: it marshals the evidence from across the educational leadership, administration and management literatures as well as that from educational law and policy studies. Also it is very readable: Gibton has the rare skill of being able to present complex ideas in a clear way and his writing style is one which grabs you and keeps your interest. The case studies for example are engaging. I just wish there had been opportunities for him to have explored the issues raised with other key stakeholders such as teachers, governors and policy makers.

The book provides many insights into what education law does to the work of headteachers of schools in England – their role, their leadership and their relations with local and national authorities. Areas discussed include admissions, performance management, league tables, inspection and the national curriculum but one area that struck me in particular concerned relations with governing bodies. The headteachers interviewed in the study are generally quite critical of this particular reform, noting how empowered governing bodies have not been fully realised. Whilst welcoming the support offered, they have to spend time on servicing and educating governors. Other research supports the contention that there is a growing gap between schools and their governing bodies, and this reflects the increasing disparity and inequality between what Gibton calls strong and weak schools. He states that equality is the one issue that needs constant and unrelenting government support or it simply will not happen.

It is headteachers who bear the brunt of educational law and who are at the crux of the implementation process but, as Gibton convincingly argues, they are not fully recognised in that process. Heads have a good understanding of law-based reform and have strong views about its hidden agendas. It is the heads' task to decipher and make sense of educational law as it is handed down to them. Gibton's case studies provide fascinating insights into how heads perceive the law and manage the implementation process. He found that heads often ignore those aspects of legislation they see as unimportant or not in line with their own values about what education is or should be about. The circumvention of laws that appears to be commonplace is perhaps a good antidote to those theorists who see headteachers as mere implementers of government policy (law) within a dominant culture of performativity and managerialism. It appears that there is still a place for 'values-driven' leadership and Gibton's study provides further evidence of this being practised. Heads' initial great respect and curiosity towards the law has waned to be replaced by shrewd politics and survival tactics. This Gibton tells us is an important warning sign for government.

The book concludes with some ideas and suggestions of possible new legislation and other actions which will help to narrow the gap between what laws want heads to do and what they can actually accomplish. Like the rest of the book these are thoughtful and helpful. At a time when urban education and the difficult task of leading schools in challenging circumstances is high on the political agenda – in England for example we have the London Challenge with its own leadership strategy – this book has much to offer and I strongly recommend it to you.

Peter Earley
Institute of Education
July 2004

Acknowledgements

I would like to thank Professor David Gillborn, formerly Head, Policy Studies Group, and Professor Sally Power, Head, School of Educational Foundations and Policy Studies (EFPS), at the Institute of Education, University of London.

I am grateful to the London Leadership Centre for its help; to the British Foreign Office for funding the fellowship at the Institute of Education, under the auspices of the Chevening Award Scholarships; and to the British Council for its administrative support.

Special thanks go to my dear hosts and friends Peter Earley and Professor Ros Levacic, from the Institute of Education, for their continuous help, advice, and contributions to this study, and to my work.

I would also like to thank Professor Nili Cohen, Rector, Tel-Aviv University, and professors David Chen and Malka Margalit, former Head and Head of the Jaime and Joan Constantiner School of Education at TAU for their help in carrying out this study, and my mentors and colleagues Professor Naama Sabar, Tel-Aviv University, and Professor Ellen Goldring, Vanderbilt University for all that I have learned from them on educational research, leadership, and policy.

Thanks to Oren Pizmoni-Levi, my dedicated and thorough research assistant, for his very good work and help.

Heaps of gratitude to the publications office at IoE: to Deborah Spring, to Brigid Hamilton-Jones, to Liz Dawn, and to Sally Sigmund – your professional and warm attitude were essential to the completion of this book.

Finally, thanks to the headteachers who dedicated some of their precious time to take part in this study. For obvious ethical reasons I cannot mention your names but you will always have a place in my heart.

A personal note: a foreigner doing research in a foreign land

On a personal note that is not disconnected from conceptual and methodological issues, all through this study, and while writing this book, I kept wondering whether being foreign is fruitful or detrimental to my research. The help I received from my English colleagues at the Institute of Education, in interpreting data and understanding the English school system was, of course, crucial to my work. I hope that examples from other countries, like the United States, as well as some from Australia and Canada and even Israel, allowed me a broad view.

I certainly enjoyed every moment.

Abbreviations

CEO	Chief Executive Officer
CTC	City Technology College
DfEE	Department for Education and Employment
DfES	Department for Education and Skills
EA	Education Act (various years: 1993, 1996, 1997, 2002)
EAZ	Education Action Zone
ERA	Education Reform Act (1988)
GM	grant-maintained
HRM	human resource management
ICT	information and communication technology
IT	information technology
LEA	local education authority
LMS	local management of schools
LPSH	Leadership Programme for Serving Headteachers
NCSL	National College for School Leadership (University of Nottingham)
NPQH	National Professional Qualification for Headship
OFSTED	Office for Standards in Education
PANDA	performance and assessment
PPP	public–private partnership
QCA	Qualifications and Curriculum Authority
s.	Section
SAT	Standard Assessment Tasks (National Curriculum tests)
SBM	school-based management
sch.	Schedule
SEN	special educational needs
SES	socio-economic status
SIA	School Inspections Act (1996)
SSFA	School Standards and Framework Act (1998)
TES	*Times Educational Supplement*
USP	Urban Systemic Program
VA	voluntary aided
VC	voluntary controlled

Introduction

The purpose of this book is to explore the links between educational law and law-based reform in England, and educational leadership. These roads, to paraphrase Frost, diverge, and this book attempts to take the one less travelled. The main point of this exploration is that educational law and law-based reform have profound influence on educational leadership and the work and professional life of school headteachers. Although this link is obvious, educational leadership, and specifically the role of school headteachers,[1] is a different domain, studied in distinct separation from educational law. This book attempts to say something on both of these fields, in a set-up where educational law and educational leadership are part of ongoing reform and debate: England's school system in the post millennium era.

Since the late 1980s, England's educational policy has been characterised by massive, widespread, and frequent legislation (Gibton and Goldring 2002; Harris 1993; Ford *et al.* 1999; Ruff 2002). The two main themes of this legislation are: first, substantial decentralisation of the system with emphasis on school autonomy and parental school choice; and second, underscoring the first, the establishment of centralised curricula, centralised standards, and centralised testing and auditing mechanisms. The two themes have enormous ramifications on the role and work of educational leaders, and are presented and analysed in this book. Law-based reform in England had two distinct stages. The first stage was between 1980 and 1996: under the Conservative government, free market choice coupled with centralised curriculum were the main themes. From 1997, under the Labour government, a regulatory role was added in an attempt to balance free market forces with a 'third way' (Giddens 1998; Whitty *et al.* 1998) of change, and to promote a social policy that aspires to more equality, local and school empowerment, accompanied by strong audit and supervision. This book will explore how headteachers feel about these two stages.

The main thesis of this book is that English educational law-based reform is unaware of the circumstances of educational leadership. Its language differs from the language of school headteachers and educational leadership, though it is this leadership, and these leaders, that are the vehicle upon which law-based reform attempts to reach its goals within educational policy. These gaps cause severe pressures on educational leaders. Most of these pressures are unnecessary and irrelevant to the targets of law-based reform. This book offers some possibilities for improving dialogue research and understanding of the implications of law-based reform for the work of headteachers.

The stories of the English headteachers featured here also present the story of educational leaders in both a decentralised and a centralised system. It is also the story of the Labour government's attempt to reshape the education system and how this attempt is viewed by headteachers – most of whom are dedicated supporters of the government, yet perhaps its strongest critics.

Plan of the book

Chapter 1 presents a short literature review on law-based reform and its socio-political aspects. The chapter includes a brief summary of law-based reform regarding decentralisation, school-based management and headship in England from 1988 to 2003. Further, it includes a brief comparison between law-based reform in the US and in the UK. Emphasis is on legislation that deals with school-based management, accountability issues, division of responsibilities among national, local, and school authorities (including governing bodies and headteachers), and types of schools that exist in both systems, all from a legal-political point of view.

Chapter 2 draws upon literature on educational leadership, administration, and management, and analyses law-based educational reform in England. Questions addressed are: What type of leadership is encouraged by English law-based reform? How are headteachers perceived, formally and informally, in legislation? Does legislation encourage the emergence and growth of middle and senior management teams within schools? How does legislation on headteacher training and nomination emphasise managerial, moral, and other streams within educational leadership? What is the image of school headteachers as it emerges from legal texts? This is done through content analysis of legislation, especially under Prime Minister Tony Blair during the period of this study (1999–2002). Qualitative methods will provide 'grounded theory' on the hidden, tacit agendas and the formal explicit and declared agendas. This chapter also attempts to say something about research on educational leadership, research on law-based reform, and on the theory that underlies both fields.

Chapters 3 and 4 present the detailed cases of eight headteachers and their schools, and one Education Action Zone (EAZ), in southeast England, concentrating on what educational law does to their work, role, leadership, and relations with local and national authorities. The cases show how headteachers tackle issues such as: catchment areas and admissions; exclusions and appeals; pupil retention and dropout rates; religious education, multicultural issues, and minority education; teacher recruitment, performance management, and assessment; school finance and budget; school inspections and audit; governing bodies and relations with the local education authority (LEA) and the Department for Education and Skills (DfES). All are analysed from a legal point of view, on the one hand, and in the light of socio-political debate on educational leadership and administration, on the other hand. Overarching issues such as social justice and distribution of public goods by law, as seen by the headteachers, will be dealt with as well. These chapters will present the case of law-based reform in England through the eyes of the headteachers. The main point is that educational law must have these educational leaders in mind, for not only are they affected by it, they are also central to the law's implementation.

Chapter 5 presents cumulative findings from a total of 29 case studies and written data gathered from 25 additional schools. These findings show that headteachers have good awareness of educational law and have strong ideas about the hidden agendas of law-based reform. The head-teachers attempt, day by day, to decipher the conundrum of educational law as it is handed down to them in great volume. They differentiate between laws they define as 'purely legal' and others they see as 'legal-political' – that is, laws whose sole purpose is to advance political plans and that might disregard everyday life and conditions in schools. The headteachers admit quite openly that they tend to circumvent laws of the latter kind. This has substantial implications for educational policy and for the chance of law-based reform actually succeeding. These cases also present views headteachers have expressed openly on educational policy in England including some on multicultural and religious education, on the teacher workforce, on Education Action Zones and similar urban renewal projects, on sixth-form colleges, and on race and ethnicity in schools. Finally, this chapter will show how educational law influences the headteacher's self-efficacy.

Chapter 6 dovetails the conceptualised analysis performed and presented in Chapters 1 and 2, with the findings presented in Chapters 3–5. It shows what law-based reform, from 1997 onwards, has done to headteachers who are, according to government, at the front line of education in England, but have serious doubts and critical views on what law and the policy that derives from it does to their work, and to their ability to perform, to recruit staff, and to run their schools. This chapter shows how hidden agendas in English school law may be able to shape life in schools, and perhaps may have already done so. Ways in which law-based reform shapes leaders and leadership will be discussed as well. Major points in this chapter include: the differentiation headteachers make between the political and legal aspects of law-based reform; educational law as a divider between strong and weak schools with emphasis on inner city schooling and the projects of urban renewal that attempt to help them; the role of legislation in the fortification and strengthening of the headteachers' position but also in distancing them from school staff in their professional journey from headteacher to principal and onward, perhaps to true Chief Executive Officer (CEO) of the school. Finally, some ideas on possible new legislation on educational leadership and the system are offered.

Chapter 7 offers some short concluding remarks and a summary, on how law-based reform in England can function differently in dealing with educational leadership and running schools by headteachers. This shows mainly which better mechanisms of accountability can offer headteachers actual policy and capacity tools that will narrow the gap between what laws want headteachers to do and what they can actually accomplish.

The methodology and plan of the study are outlined in the Appendix.

1 Law-based reform: the English version and its origins in the ethos of democracy

The origins of law-based reform: a conceptual framework

The area, or field of study, of law-based reform appeared in educational research mainly in the 1990s and mainly in the US (DeMitchell and Fossey 1997a; Heubert 1997, 1999a) and somewhat less in the UK (Harris 1993). Figure 1.1 presents the disciplinary and conceptual roots of law-based reform. The field is quite separate from the area of educational law. Educational law (sometimes referred to in the US as 'school law') is the legal field that deals with legal aspects of education (Ruff 2002; LaMorte 2002). Most of it is derived from the larger fields of constitutional and administrative law, all part of public law. From the constitutional point of view, educational law is related to issues like human and civil rights, children's rights, and also the evident relation between education, enlightenment, knowledge, and democracy. As education is a public service in most and sometimes all of its aspects, running, and finance, it is part of administrative law. Other areas of educational law are derived from civil and criminal law; for instance, issues of pupil safety that have to do with criminal and civil negligence. But educational law is, like other fields studied and taught in law faculties, about legislation and litigation.

Law-based reform is an interdisciplinary field of study, situated between law and social studies. I believe the sociological side is stronger than the legal side. Law-based reform, as a field, is interested in the sociology of how educational law is involved, overtly and covertly, in the fields of educational policy and administration. It is interested in how educational law becomes a policy tool, and how it influences structures and practice in education. It is also interested in the political aspects of educational law. The sociology of educational policy and the sociology of law are therefore related. First, in the sense that both fields are interested in the

Figure 1.1 *Law-based reform and its disciplinary, theoretical, and conceptual origins*

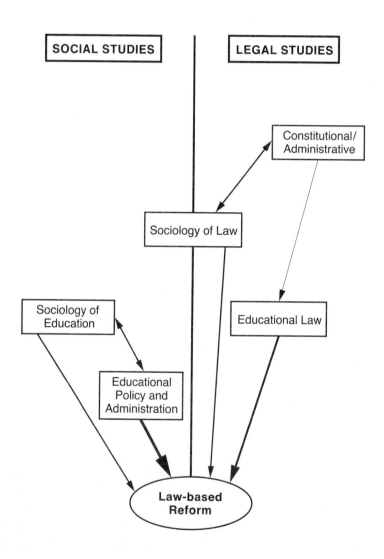

Note: Arrow widths symbolise strength of affinity.

politics of legal language and process. Second, in the sense that both fields look into the gaps between the perceived 'sacred' and 'perfect' images that law has among laypersons, and often among members of the legal and educational professions as well. This insight is often looked upon with dismay, not to say anger or perhaps despair, among large audiences. The sociology of law and the sociology of education treat educational law (Jackson 1985) and educational policy (Ball 1994; Boyd 1988; Hannaway 2004) as a type of discourse, as explained previously, and both are treated as part of politics. Educational policy and law are seen as the stronghold or perhaps last resort of any attempt to change the important field of education. The idea that law and policy can influence education a lot less than people think, and that the correlation between structures and procedures that are advanced by legislation and policy is, at best, problematic, causes an unpleasant awakening among many. So the study of law-based reform evolved from all these. This field is interested *in the seams* between law making, policy, and politics. The researchers and theoreticians in the field are usually trained in law (for understanding the unique language of law may be important) and often in social studies and/or educational administration as well. They belong to faculties of education but are also adjunct lecturers, or permanent staff, in faculties of law.

What is law-based reform – what is its role in educational policy?

Law-based reform is a term that describes statewide, large-scale national educational policy that restructures fundamental areas or parts of the system. The laws that initiate and accompany these reforms are typically very large and detailed documents, that present complete frameworks for the reform. 'Third way' politics (Giddens 1998), which appeared not only in England, advanced these law-based reforms. Typical law-based reform in the 1990s and onward included areas such as system restructuring, devolution, and redistribution of power; standards and audit mechanisms; establishing new types of schools, especially allowing schools to achieve 'charter'-type status of all sorts; school finance and funding arrangements;

national standardised curriculum; system-wide integration/desegregation, inclusion/exclusion, etc.

The idea that legislation can change the social order is based on the assumption that the law has the capability to dominate rational human behaviour (Rawls 1971; Schiff 1981). The law is the result of bargaining between groups, social institutions, and individuals, according to their relative power, and is based on the unwritten expectations and basic social norms of the particular society (Fuller 1977; Minow 1993; Rawls 1971; Tyack and Cuban 1995; Tyack *et al.* 1987). Special attention ought to be paid to the normalisation and regulation of decentralisation through legislative mandates. One naturally assumes that large-scale policy changes of such kind need some formal establishment in legislation. However, mandatory directives are successful in implementing policy especially when 'goals ... and their attainment are clear, there is a balance of public and professional support or neutrality for the change, and the target sites can feasibly achieve mandated ends' (Firestone and Corbett 1988: 325). The problem is that decentralisation is not like any other large-scale systemic change. Some conceptual problems that arise in connection with this issue are: How can legislative mandates predict the multi-variant faces of decentralisation? What is legislation's role in strengthening the 'market' aspects of decentralisation vis-à-vis the control of the 'politics' over the process (Chubb and Moe 1990)? Is legislation the opening point for implementing policy, or an 'afterthought' that attempts to regulate an already changed or changing system? Should legislation impose mandatory solutions to problems of decentralisation implementation, or should it offer optional possibilities?

Two important books (DeMitchell and Fossey 1997a; Heubert 1999a), that mark the growing interest in these questions, came out in the US in the 1990s and offer quite opposite approaches to law-based reform related issues. DeMitchell and Fossey (1997a, b) are sceptical about the benefits of using legislation as a means to control and implement decentralisation and restructuring in education. They point to two contradictory waves of reform in the US, only a few years apart. The first wave, in the late 1980s, included centralised, bureaucratic policies that focused on accountability, standards, and excellence. The second wave, from the early 1990s, focused on decentralisation, deregulation, and school, teacher, and community empowerment. In their in-depth analysis of reforms in several states (including Tennessee, Kentucky, and New York), DeMitchell and Fossey caution that

> Mandates, rules and regulations are not enough, if reform efforts are to be effective and not fall prey to the issue-attention cycle that claimed many reforms ... capacity-building policy instruments may be the more effective alternative to mandates in the long run.
>
> (DeMitchell and Fossey 1997a: 7)

In another study on charter school laws in the US, DeMitchell and Fossey found that half of over 20 states that accepted such laws indeed used legislation to ensure the true autonomy of these schools. In the other half, however, legislation was actually *eventually* used to *curb* the attempt to open many such schools and ensure they are free of centralised policy. This happened because the legislation process alerted powerful agencies, such as teachers' unions, whose pressures resulted in weakened charter school laws. Harris (1993), who wrote a comprehensive book on legislation's role in the UK's education system, and one of the first ever on law-based reform, is also quite sceptical. He points out that the vast legislation in the UK during the 1980s offered a bit more consumer control and choice in education (especially through the appeal system and publishing of league tables) but that these tools changed public control and influence over the system only marginally. A lot of law-based reform that attempted to implement market or quasi-market mechanisms (Levacic and Woods 2000; Levacic 2002; Walford 1990) assumes that a neo-classic market can exist in education (House 1996). The existence of such a framework relies on the public having all the necessary information about choice in education; having the relevant knowledge necessary for interpreting and utilising this information; having low loyalty to the product and high ability to switch from one 'supplier' to another. In practice none of these exist and certainly not among the public as a whole. Schools are an 'invested asset' and moving one's child to another school is problematic.

Even when information is abundant, the tools to evaluate it are scarce and people with higher education and more money have an advantage. So, relying on market forces to improve the system in some magical way is appealing, but not supported by hard evidence. Many law-based reforms in the US and England from the 1990s and onwards are underscored by an agenda that subsumes the possibility to create a true neo-classic market in the field. Decentralisation, standardised testing, and advertising information in several channels often constitute the content of these reforms. Legislation is used not just because of the mere fact that mandates are a tool for reform in public services. In the case of the 1990s law-based reform they are much more: first, a public proclamation of the dramatic shift in power; second, a formal act of passing power, rights, and duties, or rather franchises and entitlement, from the state to schools on the one hand, and to parents, communities, and constituencies on the other hand; and third, a new framework within which the state, the local authorities, the parents, various interest groups (e.g. religious, ethnic, ideological, business, etc.) are to operate from now on.

Heubert, who leads research and writing on law-based reform in the US, gathered in the book he edited (1999a) a formidable group of writers (such as Gary Orfield who writes on desegregation and Paul Weckstein on quality education) and researchers on the issue. His approach is much softer and more optimistic. According to Heubert, US education has benefited from the outcomes of law-based reform, and law-based reform can be an effective tool for advancing values in education. This is especially true when decentralisation and standards-based reforms are the crux of change. When equity and fairness are jeopardised, legislation may indeed be the remedy. He does, however, indicate some problems. One problem is the gap between lawmakers and educators – the gap between policy, law, and pedagogy (Reglin 1992; Weckstein 1999). Legislators tend to see the educators as conservative and outdated in the ways of the world, especially in the economic and managerial ways of thinking that are so strong these days. Educators, from their point of view, feel that policy makers have little understanding of life in schools and the constraints of their work. Heubert insists that

Poor collaboration between educators, lawyers, researchers and parents makes it difficult to use the law to advance important educational aims. Poor collaboration also leads to unnecessary lawsuits, which can cost thousands or even millions of dollars and can reduce significantly the funds that would otherwise be available for other purposes. Court orders and consent decrees, usually entered when school authorities are unwilling or unable to address problems on their own, can hamstring educators for decades, dramatically reducing discretion and flexibility in addressing central questions of education and school leadership.

(Heubert 1999b: 7)

Weckstein is also cautiously optimistic about the ability of law-based reform to bring forward fundamental changes in school reform. He offers a formula that assumes the following:

Families do care about education ... we have substantial knowledge about what it takes ... to provide it, that the authority and obligation to do so exist – and that when desire, knowledge, and authority do converge, things do happen.... The effort to draw them together is the basis for the collaboration between law and education.

(Weckstein 1999: 308)

Weckstein cautions that the problematic experiences educators have with school reform prompt them to circumvent reform as a tool for success. The increased emphasis on legislative mandates is part of the attempt by policy makers to succeed better in implementing reform and forcing educators to comply. This vicious circle should be broken – the sooner the better. So in the face of this messy situation of mutual mistrust and suspicion the solution lies in the adoption of a three-stage process that includes:

1. Stimulating demand for change by parents, aided by educators and advocates, understand what to look for in schools and their rights to obtain it; 2. Building school and staff capacity – by combining adequate resources with a committed focus on the kinds of pedagogy, curriculum-embedded assessment, teacher preparation ... supporting structures ... that the research shows stimulate high-level student learning and; 3. Enforcing accountability for implementing policy.

(Weckstein 1999: 363)

Another aspect of legislation and litigation in decentralised systems concerns the problem of unequal funding to school districts and communities. This problem had probably existed in centralised systems too, but was less self-evident. Decentralisation and autonomous schools made financial differences much more conspicuous than before. Substantive gaps in the public and private investments in education originate because communities that are more affluent can afford to dispense more funds to schools, and the schools are often managed more efficiently, anyway. A wave of litigation on unequal funding in the US had brought with it policy changes in many states, but it seems unclear whether this actually succeeded in creating a more equitable system (Goertz 1999; Pullin 1999; DeMitchell and Fossey 1997b). Measuring educational equity fiscally, not to mention pedagogically, is complex (Levacic 1995) and courts are obviously not the best place to do so.

As in other aspects of the implementation of decentralisation policy, the form and content of law-based reform differ substantially in different countries. The structure of the state, its political and legal systems, has a lot to do with these differences (Gibton *et al.* 1998). In the UK, legislation is a powerful tool that attempts to regulate educational policy. Since the late 1980s a wave of legislation has had considerable impact on Britain's educational system: school autonomy and decentralisation on the one hand, and centralised curriculum and standards evaluation on the other hand, are two of the most relevant issues that legislation in the UK has dealt with. Educational law and decentralisation have been used as weapons in the battle over the control of education between the Conservative and Labour parties (Harris 1993). This is presented in further detail in this chapter. In the US, legislation varies from one state to another, though many states have gone through similar processes (DeMitchell and Fossey 1997a). The schools in the US have had, through school boards and counties, considerable autonomy. Recent legislation is more about standards and accountability, with some attention to charter schools – mainly in the Midwestern states, e.g. Kentucky, Illinois, Wisconsin, and Missouri. In general, one could say that litigation and court rulings have played a much greater part in regulation and implementation of decentralisation policy in the US than they have in the UK – especially on the issue of equal funding. This is probably because legislation in the UK had made an initial comprehensive and centralised attempt at regulating the system as a whole, thus minimising the need for litigation. In Canada, legislation has served as a double-edged sword. On the one hand, a quasi-optional 'core curriculum' had been established – its implementation a condition for receiving public funds for schools. On the other hand, a large number of schools were granted substantial autonomy through 'charter' status (Jefferson 1996; Wayne-McKay and Sutherland 1990).

Law-based reform *is* a policy tool, and has been used frequently from the 1990s onwards, both in the US (DeMitchell and Fossey 1997b; Heubert 1999a; Pullin 1999) and in England (Harris 1993). But is it useful? The answer, as in many educational issues, is complex and will be explored further in this book.

Law-based educational reform: English and global contexts

Contradictions and opposing forces, ideas and practical models of running schools, characterised law-based reform in the 1990s. As decentralisation is the theme of most reforms in many countries, it is at the core of these contradictions. Figure 1.2 shows some of the forces that are the conceptual framework of this book (Gibton 2003).

The *first force*, along the left side of the triangle, is that of free market ideology embodied in the mechanism of accountability. The *second force*, along the right side, is that of democratisation, or what Chubb and Moe (1990) define as 'politics'. This is embodied in the idea of school autonomy. When translated into school structure, free market ideology becomes 'school-based management' (SBM). Democratisation is implemented through 'restructuring'. Brown (1990: 89) says that SBM is 'a manifestation of decentralisation'. These two forces are catalysts of law-based reform, and legislation is a primary policy tool in their implementation.

Restructuring is a realisation of the decentralisation process both in the educational system as a whole (sometimes also referred to as 'system restructuring' – Aspin and Chapman 1994) as well as within the school

Figure 1.2 *Decentralisation policy and its translation into values and structures*

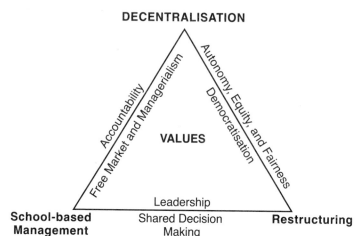

itself (referred to as 'school restructuring' or simply the 'restructured school'). It is a political and cultural phenomenon (Murphy 1993; Conley 1997), also sometimes labelled as 'reculturing' (Hargreaves 1995; Woods *et al.* 1997). Restructured schools redefine their relationships with their immediate surroundings, especially with the parents and the community, and try to take charge of educational reform. The restructured school, rooted in socio-political global 'megatrends' (Caldwell 1993), attempts to fulfil aspirations for democratisation and cultural diversity in the school system (Dellar 1994; Fullan 1991; Hallinger and Hausman 1994; Murphy 1993, 1994; Muth and Segall 1993).

The left side of the triangle in Figure 1.2 is the managerial side of, or outcome of, decentralisation policy. Despite the fact that some critiques of educational policy in England tend to put Conservative policy and the Labour policy that followed under one title, there are significant differences, relevant to the utilisation of law as a policy tool. The Conservatives emphasised the role of the market in reorganising the system and redefining targets:

> This process was based on market rules and the assumption that better quality would be achieved through freedom, autonomy and entrepreneurship, and that schools could no longer expect to have to rely solely on public funds.
>
> (Volansky 2003: 244)

Law-based reform in the Conservative era indeed attempted to create market conditions by allowing schools to 'opt out' and achieve grant-maintained status. The 1988 Education Reform Act clearly adopted a 'consumerist' approach (Harris 1993). According to Bottery, decentralisation in the 1990s differs from decentralisation in the 1980s. While in the 1980s free market forces controlled decentralisation, the 1990s are governed by managerialism. Bottery labels this phenomenon as the work of 'New Modernisers' who

> embrace the freedom of the global market; there could be no great freedom for educational providers, no return to the golden age of professional autonomy.... Money would have to be spent carefully, agendas very clearly specified and assessment/surveillance of providers would have to be very strong. There could be no room for educators 'doing their own thing'.
>
> (Bottery 2000: 34)

These ideas were and are appealing to the public because they create a posture of public control over education, a posture of choice, and a posture of 'crime and punishment'. This was a new setting in comparison to the past when the public, represented by its elected politicians, put vast amounts of money into schools with no, or very little, influence on what goes on in them, on the socio-political outcomes and outputs, especially in terms of social mobility and access to public goods and social capital. So some of the ideas of managerialism, especially the accountability-laden ones are quite fair in Rawlsian terms. If in the past schools tended to reproduce the social structure, and socio-economic background was not a starting point but rather an end or an excuse for poor results, now schools cannot use (or abuse) this background and are supposedly measured by standards of social mobility and fairness. But this left side of the triangle has a dark side as well:

This course became a deliberate policy at the expense of social cohesiveness, creating winners and losers and causing wide gaps between those institutions able to compete and those unable to do so. The application of market rules created new values and priorities in education: headteachers came to be valued for the ability to raise money and to compete in cash terms rather than in educational terms.

(Volansky 2003: 244)

The managerial ethos (Bottery 1992, 2000; Ball 1987, 2003) might ignore issues such as equity, equality, trust, and care (Bottery 2000) and reduces value-laden issues into technicalities, thus turning 'theories of organisation' into 'ideologies' (Ball 1987: 5). This again is an issue that law-based reform should, but often fails, to address (Orfield 1999; Weckstein 1999). Instead of attempting to create some form of balance between the two sides of the decentralisation triangle, legislation tends to represent the left side, swiftly imposing managerial practices and ideologies on the system while promising the public control, choice, cost-effectiveness, and fairness. The introduction of standards and audit mechanisms, that began during the Conservative government and was further amplified under the Labour government, did not reduce the negative anti-egalitarian characteristic of the managerial era (Weckstein 1999).

As research on decentralisation continued, the political, economic, and legal aspects overshadowed the pedagogical ones (Dimmock 1993; Elmore 1993; Hannaway 1993; Whitty *et al.* 1998). A substantive literature points out that decentralisation policy allows governments 'a complete abdication of responsibility by the state' (Whitty *et al.* 1998: 45), thus creating a form of insulation between the state and the education system (Weiler 1993). Therefore, notwithstanding contradictory decentralisation policy, both declared and implemented, the state re-centralises certain factors or parts of the system so it can keep some of its control (Elmore 1993; McDonnell 1989; Odden 1991) or legitimacy (Whitty *et al.* 1998). This, coupled with public concern about the performance of public education and the practical need of consumers to acquire detailed information about schools so that they can choose among them, enhanced the appearance of the 'Standards movement'. Numerous national evaluation bodies and agencies (e.g. OFSTED in the UK, NAEP in the US, and CMEC/SAIP in Canada)[1] in charge of auditing and assessing multiple aspects of school performance were established, their results published through 'league tables', 'benchmarking', government websites, and similar mechanisms (Leithwood and Aitken 1995; Levacic 1995; Lewis 1999; McLaughlin and Shepard 1995; Whitty *et al.* 1998).

Decentralisation enjoys the support of various groups that are usually on opposite sides of the public debate on, and politics of, educational policy. These include conservative and new-right free market capitalists, and small ethnic communities; authorities and teacher unions; parents and various interest groups. This is perhaps why, as decentralisation becomes stronger and more widespread, it is also realised to be a 'one-way street'-type reform. *Each time the state wants to change something in the system the only thing it can do is decentralise it even more.* However, when decentralisation begins, the preliminary support that the various groups appeared to have voiced towards it changes, sometimes dramatically. First, everybody thinks power should be decentralised *to them alone* (McDonnell 1989; Odden 1991). Local authorities and municipalities think they should govern education. Parents think the school is theirs, in accordance with the legal concept of *in loco parentis*, or simply as consumers (Harris 1993; Booth and Bussell 1999). Principals and teachers see decentralisation as a form of professional empowerment. Ethnic and religious leaders think education should advance their cultures and agendas, etc. So the 'political' factor of the implementation process becomes messy indeed. Moving on from decentralisation into restructuring and school-based management is a difficult and tricky job. Basically, there are substantial contradictions between the two: restructuring being about the socio-political aspects of decentralisation and school-based management being about the managerial ones. Decentralisation, as a concept and an ideology, as well as an actual policy, is entwined with the democratic ethos (Boyd 2004; Strike 2004). Chubb and Moe's (1990) classic work did an important job in emphasising these contradictions:

> Democratic institutions allocate decisionmaking rights by attaching
> public authority to elected and appointed positions of government – and
> by setting out rules that specify who can occupy these positions and
> how the authority attached to them must be exercised.... In this sense,
> democracy is essentially coercive. The winners get to use public
> authority to impose their policies on the losers.... What makes this
> peculiar form of coercion broadly acceptable is that public authority
> does not belong to any individual or group. It is up for grabs.
>
> (Chubb and Moe 1990: 28, 29)

So, 'politics' are a fair system in Rawlsian terms, but not necessarily a
system of choice and competition, except for elections occasionally.
According to Rawls: 'social and economic inequalities are to be arranged
so that they are both (a) reasonably expected to be to everyone's advantage,
and (b) attached to positions and offices open to all' (Rawls 1971: 60).
While Rawls emphasises the 'justice' aspect of democratic institutions,
Chubb and Moe focus on the political aspect. But basically, they describe
a similar system that is accepted because the general public sees it as fair.
Chubb and Moe's important contribution to this discussion is the distinction between 'politics' and 'markets', in which:

> Governments must create a legal framework that specifies and enforces
> property rights. They must use their public authority, in other words, to
> impose a system of rules for determining who owns what property and
> for assigning to owners the authority to make certain choices about its
> disposition.
>
> (Chubb and Moe 1990: 29)

It seems there is a general notion among people that democracy and
markets are alike, or that a free market is part of a democratic society.
Perhaps this is because democracy is often intuitively connected to 'choice'
and so are 'markets'. But putting together Chubb and Moe's analysis with
Rawls's, shows that democracy ('politics') and 'markets' are in many
ways opposed to each other. Markets are about ownership, and democracy,
according to Rawls, is about fairness. When Rawls refers to fairness, he
does refer to the system by which it is achieved or by which it can at least

be reached proximally. Chubb and Moe remain within the system. They think markets are a good way to reach fairness, for instance by using vouchers. Rawls, on the other hand, says that

> A society is well ordered when it is not only designed to advance the good of its members but when it is also effectively regulated by the public conception of justice. That is, it is a society in which (1) everyone accepts and knows that the others accept the same principles of justice, and (2) the basic social institutions generally satisfy and are known to satisfy these principles.
>
> (Rawls 1971: 5)

So putting together Rawls with Chubb and Moe produces the following picture: democracy might not always be fair and markets are not necessarily a downright manifestation of democracy.

The conflict described so far is by no means unique to England's school system. It exists in the US, in Canada, in Australia, in New Zealand, and in Israel. All these countries have the same common characteristics. First, they have a liberal ethos that wishes to advance the chances of the individual to achieve self-fulfilment and authenticity. Second, they perceive education, including its accessibility and availability, and especially higher education, as the main path towards this. Third, all these countries went through vast decentralisation processes and decentralisation is considered the useful way to achieve these aspirations. The democratic ethos, in its 'Anglo-American' version, is basic to this course of action. In the 1990s and onward, this ethos offers the following, phrased dramatically by Lewis's observation that 'the pervasive belief is that the institution is the problem and the community is the solution' (Lewis 1993: 86). According to this ethos, which some may think is somewhat naïve, or romantic, each individual is capable of utilising the tools allocated by the state to achieve the maximum level of success possible in a given society. What Lewis means is that everyone *can succeed* and if not everyone succeeds, it is because of the institution, e.g. the school and school system. The purpose of law-based reform is to attempt a proximity to this ethos. Law-based reform assumes that decentralisation, coupled with centralised regulation and audit-type supervision, is the true and successful way to achieve this ethos, at least to some extent. The use of legislation to establish and operate this system, which is common to all the countries mentioned before, is not accidental. Legislation, and especially primary legislation,[2] is the highest form in which a democratic state can address the issue of public policy, in this case in education, and is the embodiment, or personification, of the democratic ethos. The use of legislation is a statement of priority and it is also a catalyst that advances and encourages public debate on educational policy. But legislation also creates, as Weiler (1993) suggests, a form of insulation between the state and the education system. In the strong words of one English headteacher in the study that is the basis of this book: 'once the government provided education, now it provides information on education'. By this statement headteachers phrase their fear that English law-based reform has gradually created a force that abandons schools and headteachers to the benevolence of fierce and uncontrolled pressures. This tension will be explored further in this book.

However, the method or manner in which decentralisation is achieved is not uniform in the countries mentioned above. This is where they differ. One characteristic that is evident in England is the massive use of legislation in this process, legislation that manifests the attempt of English governments to reshape its education system and change its fundamentals.

Law-based reform in England: a brief historic overview and some comparative analysis

This book does not present a detailed review of law-based reform in England, but more of an overview. There is abundant literature on the laws themselves (Ford *et al.* 1999; Kaye 2001; Ruff 2002), and 'law-review' literature on decentralisation and accountability and from the 1990s on law-based reform (Arthur 1998; Booth and Bussell 1999; Bradney 1996; Harris 1996, 1999; Hyams 1997; Kaye 1998; Meredith 2000; Monk 1997; Parry and Parry 2000; Ruff 1999; Tooley 1996), as well as good 'how to' prescriptive literature for headteachers (Gold and Szemerenyi

1999). But a short overview is still appropriate, so as to lay down a base for the detailed leadership-oriented literature that follows.

Since the late 1980s, England's educational policy has been characterised by massive, widespread, and frequent legislation (Harris 1993; Ford *et al.* 1999; Ruff 2002). Table 1.1 presents the main policies of this legislation.

The main two themes of this legislation are first, substantial decentralisation of the system with emphasis on school autonomy and parental school choice; the second theme, which underscores the first, includes establishment of centralised curricula, centralised standards, and centralised testing and auditing mechanisms, the main one of which is the Office for Standards in Education (OFSTED). These two themes have had wide-ranging ramifications on the role and work of educational leaders. These themes are presented and analysed in this book.

England probably has the most legislation-based decentralisation reform among English-speaking countries, if not in the world (Ford *et al.* 1999). Beginning in 1988, the Conservative government offered schools the opportunity to 'opt out', which meant becoming a 'grant-maintained' (GM) school. Such schools were allowed to gain financial and organisational autonomy and free themselves from municipal, local education authorities' (LEAs') control. This move was congruent with the Conservative government's policy of implementing free market principles in the public sector, beginning with public health systems and followed later by education. Notwithstanding, it was also, paradoxically, an attempt to centralise the school system and strengthen the grasp of central government over schools, while lessening the power of local education authorities and granting schools' autonomy, all at once. This was achieved because schools that 'opted out', that is applied for grant-maintained status, required government approval.

Parallel to the introduction of grant-maintained schools, the compulsory national curriculum that imposed content and methods on the autonomous schools was established. This was coupled with a mechanism that increased parental school choice (Booth and Bussell 1999; Harris 1993; Kaye 1998) and open enrolment. More than ten years later,

Table 1.1 *Educational legislation regarding decentralisation school reform in England, 1988–2002*

Legislation	Type	Main contents/policy	Politics
1988 Education Reform Act (ERA)	Primary	Establishing GM schools; parental choice; establishing National Curriculum.	Conservative government wanted to weaken LEA control over schools.
1993 Education Act (EA)	Primary	Establishing OFSTED; setting funding authorities.	Re-centralisation of school inspection and control.
1996 Education Act (EA)	Primary	Establishing Key Stages 1–4 and standardised assessment of achievement in schools ages 5–16.	Attempts by the new Conservative administration (John Major) to boost schools' results and hold them accountable.
1997 Education Act (EA)	Primary	Founding the Qualifications and Curriculum Authority (QCA).	
1997 DfEE (Department for Education and Employment) White Paper *Excellence in Schools*	Proposed primary legislation	Presents 6 principles of educational policy for the Labour administration stating that 'there will be unrelenting pressure on schools and teachers for improvement' (Title 4) and 'standards matter more than structures' (Title 17).	Labour government proposes yet another revolution in educational policy that 'previews' 1998 SSFA.
1998 School Standards and Framework Act (SSFA) (and Circular 10/99 'Social Inclusion – Pupil Support')	Primary	Increasing and widening OFSTED powers (including placing schools under 'special measures'); appeal procedures regarding admissions; new policy regarding permanent exclusions including appeal procedures establishing school governing bodies; setting Education Action Zones (EAZs).	Labour government begins a fourth major policy change in a decade: government turns regulator.

Table 1.1 *continued*

Legislation	Type	Main contents/policy	Politics
1998–99 QCA publications	No statutory status	Establishing National Literacy and Numeracy strategies as part of the National Curriculum and requirements in Key Stages 1–4.	Further Labour government pressure on schools and teachers and introduction of standards.
2000/2001 Education (School Teacher Appraisal) (England) Regulations	Secondary	Establishing performance management and threshold assessment procedures.	Fulfilling the promise of relentless pressure on teachers – responsibility for educational results now lies totally within the school.
2002 Education Act (EA)	Primary	Defining the powers and structure of City Academies (formerly CTCs and specialist schools); strengthening and defining the powers of school governing bodies as the actual 'board of directors' of the school.	Strengthening the splits in England's school system: lessening the role of comprehensive schooling and strengthening the segregated and elitist trends in the post 2000 law-based reforms.

Source: Gibton and Goldring (2002).

most local education authority schools (now called 'community schools') are comparatively financially autonomous as well, while grant-maintained schools (now called 'foundation schools') are somewhat less autonomous than they were. However, the end result is that most schools in England are relatively financially free of local education authority control.

Meanwhile, the Office for Standards in Education (OFSTED), a powerful, centralised mechanism for school inspection and grading, was established in 1993 (see Table 1.1), and quickly became a major factor in the life of school headteachers throughout England (Volansky 2003). Once in about every four years each school is inspected thoroughly by a team of experts. Endless energy is dedicated to preparing for these inspections, including employing private firms, frequently staffed by ex-OFSTED officials. Schools spend substantial amounts of money on preparing for these inspections – even including, unfortunately, some fabrication of necessary documents (Ouston and Davies 1998; Gibton 2001). Since the enactment of the 1998 School Standards and Framework Act (SSFA), OFSTED has received increased powers to place schools on 'special measures' (the educational equivalent of appointing an official receiver to a liquidated company), and even to replace the headteacher with an OFSTED-appointed 'superhead' for a limited period (Harris 1996). Further centralised curriculum requirements were introduced in 1998 too, known as numeracy and literacy strategies, that focus on mathematics and English together with further testing in four age groups between ages 4–16 (known as Key Stages 1–4). All this has been accompanied by growing transparency of the evaluation and standards systems to the public, including league tables of schools that are published in the educational supplements of major newspapers and websites that present Performance and Assessment reports (PANDAs).

In the beginning of 2000, the final policy innovation of performance management and threshold assessment began to address the teacher salary system. This latest stage of educational decentralisation policy allows principals to allocate large sums of money to some teachers according to part government-based and part school-based criteria. This new policy prompted schools to establish elaborate assessment procedures to monitor teachers' work.

Politically, this law-based revolution of UK policy began during the Conservative era between the 1980s and the mid-1990s. However, the New Labour government, drawing upon 'third way' social theories (Giddens 1998), actually strengthened, widened, and deepened decentralisation policies established by the Conservatives, but, as explained beforehand, Labour added tight government control and regulation to free market mechanisms introduced by the Conservatives (Bottery 2000). When the Labour government came to power, in 1997, it published a White Paper[3] titled *Excellence in Schools* that announced 'standards matter more than structures', 'policies will be designed to benefit the many, not just the few', 'unrelenting pressure on schools and teachers for improvement', 'zero tolerance towards underperformance', and 'intervention will be in inverse proportion to success'. This legal policy paper was influenced by the idea that both education and the economy in the United Kingdom were threatened by competition from 'Pacific Rim countries' that 'do not rely on market forces alone in education and neither should we'.

The 1997 White Paper produced in its aftermath a barrage of educational legislation, and changed England's school system dramatically, continuing on the path set by the Conservative governments. Quite paradoxically, in its strive for further decentralisation, New Labour moved away from comprehensive secondary education, which had been introduced in the beginning of the 1970s, when Margaret Thatcher was Education Minister for four years, and of course continued during her years as Prime Minister. The resultant changes include widespread school diversification. Several types of schools have emerged that add segregation[4] to the English educational system. These include grammar schools – elitist, state-financed, secondary schools that handpick students from affluent neighbourhoods. Other schools are religious, most of which are Roman Catholic (RC) and Protestant (CE – Church of England) but new types (Parker-Jenkins 1998) such as Greek Orthodox (Johnson 2003) began appearing in small numbers that may point towards a developing tendency. Especially interesting are Education Action Zones (EAZs) established under the School Standards and Framework Act of 1998 (Gillborn 1998) that focus on public–private partnerships (PPPs). The goal is to form alliances between large private companies and public money in urban renewal projects that include a whole-school (Fullan 1991; Sarason 1982) or rather a whole-neighbourhood or a whole-borough educational system change. In order to receive these grants schools are required to come together and present grant applications, as part of what is called 'bid culture' (Gibton 2001).

Another type of school that emerged is 'specialist schools'. These are former comprehensive high schools that have excelled in several areas, including academic achievement and organisational matters, as determined by an OFSTED audit, and have developed a curricular speciality (e.g. science education, arts). By obtaining 'specialist' status, these schools receive extra funds and are partially allowed to choose some (between 10 and 30 per cent) of their students according to academic excellence. The extra funds are used for promoting the school's educational targets and helping other schools in their improvement attempt. City Technology Colleges (CTCs), that existed under the Conservative government as well, finalise this spectrum of niche-type 'magnet' schools, which received formal recognition in the Education Act 2002.

Law-based reform under the Labour government peaked between 1998 (SSFA 1998) and 2002 (EA 2002) in two important areas. The first is the strengthening of governing bodies that are now formally in charge of supervising the running of schools. The second is threshold assessment and performance management that substantially increase differential wages for teachers who show ability and outcomes and empower headteachers in the area of teachers' wages.

2 The leadership agenda of English law-based reform

Plan of chapter: analysis of legal text through the language of educational administration and leadership

The first part of this chapter offers a conceptual framework of the fields of educational administration and leadership and their links to educational policy and law-based reform. This part includes methodological issues of the research of educational policy and educational administration – attempting to explore why these areas, which were linked so closely in the past, have gradually drifted apart. Drawing upon the most recent work from the US and England, the chapter highlights the organisational factors necessary for educational leaders in order for them to implement the relevant and essential parts of law-based reform successfully. This first part will also explore the specific conditions within schools and within systems that can facilitate successful implementation – all these from a school leadership viewpoint.

The second part of the chapter analyses several pieces of primary legislation that were accepted by Parliament under the Labour government from 1997. These laws were analysed in a constant comparative method (Charmaz 2000; Hutchinson 1988; Strauss 1987; Strauss and Corbin 1994). Content analysis included two separate stages. First, legislation was analysed and cut into what are known as 'emic' categories – categories obtained from the raw material that is analysed as is. Second, legislation was analysed using 'etic' categories – those categories brought from outside, e.g. from theory or previous research, and used to 'cut' the material according to these external parameters, variables, or concepts. In this study, the 'etic' categories were based on Adams and Kirst's (1999) model of accountability and on Glatter's (2002) model of governance. The main material that was the core of the analysis in this study included

the School Standards and Framework Act (SSFA 1998) and the Education
Act 2002 (EA 2002), which are the two major pieces of primary legislation
enacted by the Labour government since 1997. In addition, several policy
documents that are legislation-based were analysed as well. These include
the DfEE *Education Action Zone Handbook* (issued October 1998), the
National Standards for Headteachers (NCSL Draft Consultation document, September 2003), the DfES circular and regulations regarding
Performance Management in schools (issued September 2001), and School
Governance Regulations (issued in 2003). These important and extensive
laws and legal instruments represent the essence of law-based reform in
England since the Labour government came to power in 1997. Some
legislation from the previous Conservative government was analysed as
well, because a substantial part of law-based reform under the Labour
government is founded on that enacted by the Conservative government.
The Conservatives, in their turn, also legislated massively on education,
beginning with the formidable Education Reform Act (ERA 1988) and
onwards (EA 1993 and 1996). Finally, ten editions of the *Times Educational Supplement* (TES) spread chronologically between the years 2000
and 2003 were analysed. The material was chosen because it throws a
contemporary light onto the English educational arena and shows some
of what is going on in the field. Research in schools and among school
headteachers will be presented in Chapters 4, 5, and 6.

Educational policy, educational administration, and educational leadership: worlds drifting apart?

As explained in Chapter 1, decentralisation is both an ideology and a
policy tool. The gap between the democratic right side of the model in
Figure 1.2 and the managerial left side is a main theme in this book. I aim
to show that the tension between these two 'sides' of decentralisation,
manifested in England's law-based reform, is not really solved or lessened
by it but rather is a difficult issue passed on to headteachers to confront.
Legislation is often the means by which decentralisation is planned and
enforced, while educational administration is the domain in which it

operates, and educational leadership is essential to fulfil it. However, the two areas grow out of very different disciplines (i.e. law, and educational administration), and use completely different languages, which are spoken by different experts in academia, among practitioners, and among policy makers. Although the terms 'administration' and 'management' initially and essentially include the role of law in education, in practice this is not the case. This can be demonstrated by the split in the American Educational Research Association (AERA), the largest educational research organisation in the world (Gibton 2004), which is truly international and encompasses researchers from numerous nations, countries, fields of study, and academic and other educational institutions. The split is in Division A (titled 'Administration') from which emerged Division L (titled 'Policy'). While the original Division A included all aspects of educational administration, including in-school administration and system-wide management and policy, now these two areas are divided into the two divisions. This is a bit theoretical. In practice, Division A does indeed emphasise educational leadership and in-school administration, but also deals with system-wide issues. Division L focuses on system-wide issues that also include educational law and economics in education. These latter two are distinctly part of Division L, and are relatively new. The split is the end, not the beginning, of a process that eventually produces the two 'languages' mentioned beforehand.

The field of educational and law-based reform is controlled by legal theory and legislative practice. It perceives educational policy, and public policy in general, in linear terms. This linear approach is underlined by positivist philosophy. Positivism, despite being gradually criticised and downsized in the past two decades or so (Hammersley and Gomm 2002; Popkewitz 1999a), is still a mainstream point of view in educational policy. The outcome of the positivist base of educational policy is an approach that assumes educational reality as a set of separate variables that can be controlled separately in the field. This approach, which is at the heart of educational policy and law-based reform, gradually distances these two important fields from the field of educational leadership. All this happens while research cautions that strengthening the links between inner-school administration and system, or statewide policy, is necessary for understanding what educational leadership is today (Bell and Bush 2002; Foskett 2003). Policy studies are not supplied with a strong enough foundation of knowledge, and the conceptual and methodological rift between studies on law-based reform and on decentralisation is a sad example. Research on policy, caution Cizek and Ramaswamy (1999), is crisis-oriented in its findings but not solution-oriented enough. Tough times require new, multi-paradigmatic ideas, tools, and frameworks if research is to offer new ideas for policy makers (Biddle and Anderson 1990; Finn 1990; Kennedy 1999; Levin 1990). Until this happens, policy retains its 'messy' (Kennedy 1999: 58) quality as something that is very difficult, if at all possible, to study.

Educational leadership is a field of study with origins in organisational theory, industrial and organisational psychology, educational sociology, organisational sociology, and business administration. The study of educational leadership has evolved from being part of leadership research in general, in which leadership was perceived as universal, standardised, and typical (Gibton 2003), to leadership that is perceived as dependent on context, situation, politics, and culture. Up-to-date research emphasises the unique qualities of educational leadership, but also maintains strong ties with the universal, psychological, and business origins of leadership (Davies 2003; Davies and Davies 2003b). The methodology of research on educational leadership also went through change, which was congruent with the paradigmatic change from universalism to context-laden leadership. This meant a paradigmatic shift from quantitative methods that utilise survey-type large-scale research and deductive and inferial statistical analysis, to qualitative small-scale case study type research that aims for grounded theory. Educational policy is still studied through positivist research. So gradually, the two languages evolve, and go separate ways. Popkewitz (1999a) describes this situation as a room with two ends:

> At one end of the room and taking up the most space are the various groups of people who practice a pragmatic empiricism. They are concerned with 'useful' knowledge and spend a lot of time talking about the procedures of measurement and the rules for collecting data. The

pragmatic empiricists believe that better rationalization and administration of institutions can produce social progress.... at the different end of the room ... are different groupings of 'critical' researchers. This part of the room is concerned with how existing relations can be interrogated to understand issues of power and institutional contradictions. The 'critical' research empirically investigates how schools work, but that interest focuses on problems of social inequity and injustice produced through the practices of schooling.

(Popkewitz 1999a: 3–4)

This dichotomous and conflictual approach is somewhat true but seems to be too extreme. Is there no way to reconcile the two ends of the room? Are all researchers divided so sharply? This book attempts to say that while addressing the political and critical aspects of educational policy and administration and the research on these issues is important, stating that all policy makers are socially indifferent and insensitive positivists is wrong. On the contrary, what is needed is dialogue between ends of the room to improve and deepen perspectives on education (Gibton 2004). Torres, too, provides useful insights with his work on policy analysis:

The obsession of mainstream analysts and government officials with efficiency has led to an understanding of the constraints (or restraints) on policymakers' actions, and particularly the importance of issues of class, race, and gender. In short conventional studies on policy making (inspired by the rational paradigm of educational administration), on incrementalist perspectives, and/or structural-functionalist approaches, lack the theoretical sophistication needed to understand a rather complex and rather sophisticated political process of public policy making in capitalist advanced and dependent societies. The importance of critical theory informing a political sociology of education lays in its theoretical impetus, which suggests a dual, mutually inclusive and interactive focus on the structural constraints of human action, and on the historicity of human relations.

(Torres 1999: 95)

Hammersley also points to what he calls a 'one worldism' trend in educational policy analysis in which 'the activity of research feeds directly and smoothly into practice' (Hammersley 2002: 77). However, while I agree that these distinctions exist, the alienation between these separate approaches is not useful. Some researchers distance themselves from policy and retain a constant critical approach to everything government does. This approach perhaps has roots in Marxist and neo-Marxist theory that is suspicious towards practically any form of government. Perhaps what is needed is more multi-paradigmatic and multi-method research that can provide the needs of policy makers and critical researchers at the same time to produce equitable and implementable policies that do con-sider the non-linear quality of policy and administration. Some research of this type can be found in Levacic's (1995) work on locally managed schools; Goldring and Rallis's (1993) on principals in dynamic schools; and Gillborn and Youdell's (2000) work on educational policy in England and its implications for equity in schools. What is common to all of these, is utilisation of both large-scale quantitative data with in-depth small-scale case studies that offer interpretation of statistical information and better understanding of the intricate way in which policy affects life in schools and the life of headteachers and educational leaders (Gibton 2004). This type of work, coupled with theoretical analysis of research on policy and administration (Ball 1994; Hammersley 2002; Popkewitz 1999b; Torres 1999; Whitty *et al.* 1998), produces new insights such as:

> policy making is now viewed as a much more complicated and messy process, one that involves continual negotiation, redefinition, and tinkering rather than one that involves selecting from among clearly defined alternatives one that best matches a clearly defined goal.
>
> (Kennedy 1999: 58)

The disciplinary and theoretical framework within which this research is carried out has also changed from work that was heavily inclined towards psychology (organisational and industrial) and later towards business administration, to work that is much more sociological, philo-sophical, and lately quite original in its theory (Gibton 2003). Research methods have changed as well, from quantitative experimental, to quali-tative field-oriented small sample case studies based heavily on personal reflections and narrative-style studies. These latter types of work are not the ones that catch the eye of policy makers and lawmakers who, rightly perhaps, find it difficult to inculcate and incorporate these studies in their view of education. This is also because education is such an enormous public arena with hundreds of thousands of employees and multi-billion budgets – probably the most all-engulfing public service of our time, a service that actually delivers a *complex professional public good to all the citizens every day*, much more so than health, policing, and welfare, which are delivered to only a small portion of the public at any given time. In fact, drinking water and sewerage are much more equivalent in their daily dispersion, but of course are more technical and easy to manage and control. The educational policy makers are perhaps suspicious of small-scale reflective research on educational leadership and simply speak different languages. It is also understandable that in a statistics-based 'positivist' society it is quite intimidating to reach systemic, long-range, and expensive decisions based on small sporadic samples. In this sense, the study presented in this book is somewhat problematic as well – though some steps have been taken to correct this (see Appendix, and also Gibton 2004). The vicious circle turns and turns, as the relatively small-scale, qualitative research on educational leadership shuts itself further off, and educational policy relies on work that deals with other issues. Of course, not all work is like this. Some studies attempt to combine qualitative and quantitative work and reach large and diverse audiences. One impressive example is the report on the 'state of school leadership in England' by Peter Earley and his colleagues (2002) from the Institute of Education at the University of London. Their data were gathered through quantitative methods, including many hundreds of questionnaires returned from headteachers, prospective headteachers, deputy heads, members of management teams in schools, members of governing bodies, and LEA officials, and qualitative tools which included telephone interviews with headteachers and members of management teams, focus groups, and extensive case studies in ten schools from which data were collected from headteachers, teachers, and governors, through interviews and document analysis.

The changing landscape of educational leadership

Educational leaders are going through a dramatic change in their role and professional life. Basically, the deal within which they operate is new. While in the past, headteachers were in charge of controlling their schools largely in isolation from the world outside, nowadays the school has become transparent (Meyer *et al.* 1983). The headteacher now cannot, nor wishes to, insulate the school's staff, and the school's pedagogical work, from outside interference – in other words, from the politics of education. This situation is worldwide and is reported by researchers in England (Davies and Ellison 1997; Earley *et al.* 2002; Bush *et al.* 1993; Bell and Bush 2002), in the US (Goldring and Rallis 1993; Seashore-Louis and Murphy 1994; Smrekar 1996), in Australia (Caldwell 2002), in New Zealand (Wright 2002), in Hong Kong (Cheng 2000), and in Israel (Gibton *et al.* 2000). The 'new deal' of educational management is that headteachers are accountable in relation to the fundamentals and dilemmas of the education system (Goldring and Greenfield 2002; Ogawa *et al.* 1999). Under the 'old deal', the headteacher was exempt from certain moral and educational dilemmas. As part of the 'provider controlled' system (Bottery 2000) society allowed schools nearly complete discretion on educational issues. In this 'old deal', the headteachers' role was one of preservation and continuity. Their job was to assure the teachers' protection from interference behind the classroom door and to provide professional backing for their decisions. Schools and headteachers enjoyed high status, were granted wide discretion, and were perceived as the ultimate authority on personal and intellectual potential. Socio-political tools like the eleven-plus and similar tests in other countries were seen as objective mechanisms for locating potential human growth. All this has changed, perhaps paradoxically, because the public has slowly become more educated and aware of the socio-politics of education and social mobility.

The postmodern social condition (Hargreaves 1995) includes growing awareness of the rule of institutions and growing suspicion towards the democratic state and its leading politicians, who are no longer viewed, as once they were, as the true guardians of public interest. The fact that civil identity is being pushed aside in favour of ethnic, religious, gender, and other identities opened the schools as an area of growing debate on the practices and contents of education. The headteacher is in the midst of all this. Therefore, the 'new deal' opens up schools to public scrutiny and inspection. Headteachers are measured by completely juxtaposed values and achievement variables than they were measured by during the 'old deal'. The outstanding headteacher is a 'social advocate' and a 'moral agent' (Murphy and Beck 1994: 11–13), and a large part of his or her work is in politics (Conley and Goldman 1994; Gibton *et al.* 2000; Goldring and Greenfield 2002) and marketing. The headteachers' capacity to open their schools to the general public, and transform them into something different from other schools, is essential to the schools and their survival. The introduction of decentralisation, accountability mechanisms, standards, open enrolment, and school choice all contributed to this change. As pointed out before, this happened simultaneously in many countries with 'glocal' or 'creole' versions in each different one (Bottery 2000, 2003). But headteachers also became much more interested in educational policy, specifically, and public policy and welfare policy, in general. Headteachers began asking themselves hard questions about the fundamental arrangements of education and the reciprocal influence of education and society, social justice, exclusion, and power. It is interesting that this debate emerged especially when headship turned towards managerialism. This situation has changed the way in which we look at educational leadership (Gibton 2003). The 'new deal' of educational leadership has added peril and anxiety to the work of headteachers in most countries in the Organisation for Economic Co-operation and Development (OECD) (Ackerman and Maslin-Ostrowski 2002; Barth 1986; Beaudin *et al.* 2002; Clark-Lindle 2002; Weindling and Earley 1987; Zelman and Bryant 2002), anxiety that subsequently seeped down to their management teams (Gold and Evans 2002; Wright 2002) and their teachers (Ball 2003; Hargreaves 1995; Woods *et al.* 1997). The report mentioned before, on the state of leadership in England (Earley *et al.* 2002), exemplifies the applicability of the 'new deal' concept to English school leadership as it does in many other countries. English school leaders are moving from being 'headteachers' to becoming 'principals' and perhaps even 'Chief Executive Officers' (CEOs) of schools (Glatter 2002, 2003; Levacic 2002; Leithwood *et al.* 1999; Leithwood and Steinbach 2003). The report confirms what has been found in other countries regarding the complexity of the arena within which headteachers operate, and the growing awareness and importance of politics and marketing in the headteacher's role. Their life and work have expanded and filled with new figures, bodies, and roles. In the past, they faced inwards towards their staff and students. Now they face outwards for a large portion of their time and attention – toiling at presenting the school to external agencies, gathering funds and resources, promoting programmes, building coalitions, and identifying adversaries.

The main tool that headteachers can rely on for contesting the 'new deal' situation is the adoption of new management techniques and new leadership styles. Basically, this means moving from low-order leadership, for example based on bartering, to higher-order transformational leadership based on building mutual visions with teachers and with the community (Sergiovanni 1994, 1995, 2002; Seashore-Louis and Murphy 1994; Murphy 2002). It also means developing and adopting much more complex structures that combine inner-school management and leadership with outer-school advocacy, marketing, and politics. This is quite opposite from what was required during the 'old deal'. Previously, boundaries between the inner and outer circles of schooling and educational administration were defined more accurately; retaining these boundaries was, contrary to the current 'new deal', at the essence of headship (Goldring and Greenfield 2002). Strengthening what Goldring and Greenfield call the 'stewardship of public trust' (Goldring and Greenfield 2002: 5) is at the crux of these actions by the headteacher. To do this, the headteacher should cultivate a complex structure among school staff, with numerous duties that are no longer only about running 'chunks' of the school (such as year- or cluster-heads) or pedagogical responsibilities (such as heads of departments, SEN co-ordinators, etc.). The 'new deal' infrastructure requires that political, marketing, and public relations duties be assigned to staff members, to enable the headteacher to focus much more than before on legal and financial aspects. Another important side to the managerial scene are the moral and social aspects of leadership:

> Fostering new understandings and beliefs about diversity and inclusive practice involves more than simply communicating particular understandings so that they become diffuse through an educational context ... a key strategy available to school principals for accomplishing this is the promotion of democratic discourse within the school community.
>
> (Riehl 2000: 61)

Headteachers have a 'think policy' and not just a 'think education' or a 'think management and administration' attitude. In the past, headteachers were exempt from policy issues – as policy was rigid for many years in a row and the headteachers were pallbearers of conservativism anyway. Now headteachers busy themselves with issues of equity versus competition and excellence, social justice versus capitalism, and globalisation versus multiculturalism. As headteachers become leaders not only of their schools, but also of their immediate communities, they have to broaden their horizons to understand and control issues of policy in their close vicinity. To do so headteachers have to organise their schools differently, and to familiarise their staff, and especially their deputies and their senior and middle management teams, with the contents of the 'new deal'. Schools cannot 'handle themselves as they go along'. They have to be outstanding. Headteachers are required to locate and confront 'critical success factors' (Chatwin 2003: 1) and 'capacity to improve' (Gray and Reynolds 1996), including through school-based evaluation (Nevo 1995) that equips them with 'home-made' trustworthy data.

This situation is not unique to England (Friedman 2003; Prestine 2000; Smith and Pielle 1997). Friedman, who studied 30 schools, their headteachers, and their staff in Israel, found that contemporary headteachers are constantly dealing with issues of values and politics, entwined with managerial issues and decision making. He identified three main dilemmas. The first dilemma is whether decision making is internal or compliant with external pressures. Equity-minded principals commit themselves to social justice and tend not to follow strong political and social trends that naturally benefit the few, the educated, and the affluent. The second dilemma is between egalitarianism and elitism. While the first may be just right, the second may work for the school. The third dilemma is between conservation and change. Some research (Calhoun 2002; Davies and Gold 2002; Prestine 2000) on educational administration leadership and policy shows how important law-based reform is for influencing which practices, structures and leadership styles are adopted by head-teachers. Some important factors are: a clear sense of purpose and stability, significance of local contexts in every reform, understanding the links between one reform and another, both horizontally and longitudinally, systematic building of capacity tools, the trivial link between mandatory requirements and resources, partnerships with universities and experts working alongside headteachers, providing specific and detailed information on how law-based reform is expected to improve teaching–learning practices and outcomes (Caldwell 2000; Harris 2004).

The landscape of educational law and the language of educational leadership

Educational law has reshaped the basic arrangements and structure of the education system. Table 2.1 presents an analysis of post-1996 educational law in England. These findings show that during the Labour government the decentralisation process initiated by the previous Conservative government has been halted, or rather balanced, by strong centralised processes.

However, centralisation has not necessarily brought stability in its wake. One interesting example is that even the names and titles of various components of the English system change quite often. For instance, the name of the ministry of education has changed four times in a decade from DES (Department for Education and Science) to DFE (Department for Education), then to DfEE (Department for Education and Employment), and finally to the current DfES (Department for Education and Skills – valid at the time this book is written). The same happens with schools (for instance LEA schools are now called community schools and grant-maintained schools are now called foundation schools). Some of these changes are cosmetic, and some are more fundamental, but they all add chaos to a law-based system that is supposed to be stable, at least where primary legislation is concerned.

Looking at past educational law, after 1985 one can observe a gradual process of whole system change: the strengthening of centralised initiatives and establishment of educational standards in important subjects – first the National Curriculum and later Key Stages in 1993 and Numeracy and Literacy policy in 2000; the establishment of governing bodies for *all* schools, with statutory definitions and powers; and the restrengthening of LEAs, perhaps in an attempt to balance their weakening in the late 1980s through the establishment of grant-maintained schools (Levacic 1995; Bush *et al.* 1993). What is missing is similar attention to headteachers, which is significant. After all, who more than they are responsible, are pivotal, and play a crucial role in these reforms? Why does the government think that they are the only group that does not require empowerment?

The issues that the law defines for the Secretary of State, the LEAs, and the governing bodies, are quite different in substance, scope, and language, than the issues defined for headteachers. The law regarding the first three uses broad terms such as 'to promote high standards', for instance:

> **6.** – (1) Every local education authority shall prepare an education development plan for their area, and shall prepare further such plans at such intervals as may be determined by or in accordance with regulations.
>
> **26.** – (1) Every local education authority shall prepare a school organisation plan for their area, and shall prepare further such plans at such times as may be prescribed.
>
> (SSFA 1998)

Contrary to this, the issues left to headteachers are defined in specific, narrow terms, such as 'decisions on exclusions', 'provide information',

> **69.** – (1) Subject to section 71, in relation to any community, foundation or voluntary school –

Table 2.1 *Legislation as a strengthening or weakening tool*

weakening one or two

Domain/level	DfES	LEA	School governing body	School staff	Pupils' parents	Headteacher
DfES				Power of Secretary of State to direct closure of schools, SSFA 1998 s.19		
LEA	Adjudicators appointed to modify organisation plan, SSFA 1998 s.26 Duty to publish plans for establishment of new community/foundation schools, SSFA 1998		Secretary of State's power on disputes between LEAs and gov. bodies, EA 1996 s.495 Secretary of State's power to solve disputes within LEAs, with gov. bodies, (same)			Compliance with health and safety directions, SSFA 1998 39(3)(b) Employment of head and staff by LEA in community and VA schools, EA 2002 c32 s.35 Head cannot be member of LEA appeal procedure, SSFA 1998

s i d e s

			sch.24(1)
		LEA's power to establish complaint procedures, EA 1996 s.409	Power to initiate school inspections, SIA 1996 s.25
		Gov. bodies duty to appoint staff in community schools, SSFA 1998 s.54–55	Power of intervention in maintained schools after inspection (SIA 1996), SSFA s.15
	Consultation with gov. bodies of community, foundation and VA schools, EA 1996 315 (2)		Responsibility for conduct of maintained school and achieving high standards, and annual targets, SSFA 1998 s.38, s.61, s.63
Admissions authority, SSFA 1998 s.88 and appeals s.94	Provide information and training, EA 2002 c32 s.23		Choose a baseline assessment scheme if the
School governing body			

Table 2.1 *continued*

Domain/level	DfES	LEA	School governing body	School staff	Pupils' parents	Headteacher
		Establishing school code of practice, EA 1996 s.313 2b Responsibility for maintenance of schools, SSFA 1998 s.22 Approving government instruments, SSFA 1998 sch.12				headteacher fails to do so, EA 1997 s.16 Gov. body's responsibility to do anything necessary for the conduct of the school, SSFA 1998 sch.11
School staff		Employing staff in community, VA/VC, foundation schools, SSFA 1998 s.54-55				

Pupils' parents	LEA duty to provide sufficient schooling, EA 1996 s.14(1) Appeals admissions procedure, SSFA 1998 s.94 And appeals against permanent exclusions, s.67	Duty to establish complaint procedure, EA 2002 s.29		Ensuring parents' participation in gov. bodies, SSFA 1998 9 (3)
Headteacher	Responsibility for implementation of the National Curriculum, EA 1996 s.357	Duty of LEA to provide school organisation plan, SSFA 1998 s.26	Duty of gov. body to establish complaint procedure, SSFA 1998 s.39(3)(b) Duty to consult with head before appointing administrative	Head's authority to detain, EA 1996 s.550 ... and exclude pupils, SSFA 1998 s.64–65	Head's responsibility for discipline and preventing bullying, SSFA 1998 s.61

Table 2.1 *continued*

Domain/level	DfES	LEA	School governing body	School staff	Pupils' parents	Headteacher
			staff members, SSFA 1998 sch.16 20 (3)			
			Recommending head to LEA, SSFA 1998 sch.16 7 (1)		Head's responsibility to provide information to parents, EA 1996 s.408	
			Head's duty to appear before gov. body and accept directions re: permanent exclusion, SSFA 1998 s.66			
			Establishing and implementing programmes on sex education,			

Strengthening one or two sides

EA 1996 s.404; collective worship, SSFA 1998 s.69–70; and political indoctrination, EA 1996 s.407	
Establish a balanced and broadly based curriculum, EA 1996 s.351	
Headteacher as member of gov. body, EA 1996 s.225; SSFA 1998 sch.9	
Head's duty to report to gov. body, SSFA 1998 s.42	

Notes: EA: Education Act; SSFA: School Standards and Framework Act; ER: Education Regulations; s.: section; sch.: schedule; gov.: governing; head: headteacher.

(a) the local education authority and the governing body shall exercise their functions with a view to securing, and

(b) the head teacher shall secure,

that religious education is given in accordance with the provision for such education included in the school's basic curriculum by virtue of section 352(1)(a) of the Education Act 1996.

(SSFA 1998)

The following section is a good example. In some parts, the headteacher is mentioned with the governing body and the LEA. But the phrasing (see for instance ss. 1 and ss. 6) regarding the first two, is soft, inconclusive, and phrased in future tense. The parts regarding headteachers alone (see ss. 8) are much more strict and all about '*securing that the head teacher complies with any regulations made under this section*'.

408. – (1) Regulations may require, in relation to every maintained school, the local education authority, the governing body or the head teacher to make available either generally or to prescribed persons, in such form and manner and at such times as may be prescribed –

(a) such information (including information as to the matters mentioned in subsection (2)) relevant for the purposes of any of the relevant provisions of this Part, and

(b) such copies of the documents mentioned in subsection (3), as may be prescribed.

(2) The matters referred to in subsection (1)(a) are –

(a) the curriculum for maintained schools,

(b) the educational provision made by the school for pupils at the school and any syllabuses to be followed by those pupils,

(c) the educational achievements of pupils at the school (including the results of any assessments of those pupils, whether under this Part or otherwise, for the purpose of ascertaining those achievements), and

(d) the educational achievements of pupils at such categories of school as may be prescribed (including results of the kind mentioned in paragraph (c)).

(3) The documents referred to in subsection (1)(b) are –

(a) any written statement made by the local education authority under section 370,

(b) any written statement made by the governing body in pursuance of provision made under section 371,

(c) any written statement made by the governing body of their policy as to the curriculum for the school, and

(d) any report prepared by the governing body under section 161 or paragraph 7 of Schedule 23 (governors' annual reports).

(4) For the purposes of subsection (1) the relevant provisions of this Part are … –

(5) before making any regulations under this section, the Secretary of State shall consult any persons with whom consultation appears to him to be desirable.

(6) Regulations under this section shall not require information as to the results of an individual pupil's assessment (whether under this Part or otherwise) to be made available to any persons other than –

(a) the parents of the pupil concerned,

(b) the pupil concerned,

(c) in the case of a pupil who has transferred to a different school, the head teacher of that school,

(d) the governing body of the school, or

(e) the local education authority;

and shall not require such information to be made available to the governing body, the head teacher or the local education authority except where relevant for the purposes of the performance of any of their functions.

(7) Regulations under this section may authorise local education authorities, governing bodies and head teachers to make a charge (not exceeding the cost of supply) for any documents supplied by them in pursuance of the regulations.

(8) In relation to any maintained school, the local education authority and the governing body shall exercise their functions with a view to securing that the head teacher complies with any regulations made under this section.

(EA 1996)

The language of the law, when dealing with the Secretary of State, the LEAs, and the governing bodies, uses broad policy terms, as opposed to the language that deals with headteachers, as if there were two distinct and separate 'lanes' in which legislation defines the boundaries and contents of England's school system. In the first 'lane', primary legislation offers new arrangements that are mainly about what goes on *outside* the schools. In the second 'lane', regulations and DfES directives and various other documents shape what goes on *inside* schools, especially regarding leadership and structures. This anomaly leaves headteachers behind in the changing scene of the system. This is also true where the law deals with certification:

> **6.** – (1) At any school or further education institution there shall be employed a staff of teachers suitable and sufficient in numbers for the purpose of securing the provision of education appropriate to the ages, abilities, aptitudes and needs of the pupils or students having regard to any arrangements for the utilisation of the services of teachers employed otherwise than at the school or further education institution in question.
>
> (2) Without prejudice to the generality of paragraph (1) –
>
> (a) the staff of teachers employed at a school shall include a head teacher;
>
> (b) the staff of teachers employed at a further education institution shall have qualifications appropriate to the giving of adequate instruction in the subjects in which courses are provided.
>
> (3) The requirement in paragraph (1) is additional to the requirements relating to qualifications for employment at schools contained in Part IV of these Regulations.
>
> (Statutory Instrument No. 543 The Education (Teachers)
> Regulations 1993)

According to regulation 6 (2), every school staff should include a headteacher. First, this depicts the headteacher as some kind of object. Second, the headteacher does not have any necessary qualifications, above and in addition to the detailed qualifications required from all types of teachers (SI 543 reg. 12–16, sch. 1–3). More recent regulations (SI 3111 Education (Head Teachers' Qualifications) (England) Regulations 2003) establish mandatory headship training programmes (known as NPQH). But aside from these, headteachers should be part of the teaching staff; beyond that qualifications and demands are purely administrative, i.e. that the head-teacher be appointed by the proper authority, such as the LEA, the governing body, etc. Legislation does not mention anything about the general responsibilities of a headteacher. Notwithstanding, the new National College for School Leadership, located at the University of Nottingham, has published a temporary draft of National Standards (NCSL 2003). This is indeed an impressive document but it is far from becoming part of legislation and it is doubtful whether it ever will. The standards highlight and emphasise the lack of legal formalisation, but do little to actually empower school leaders. The standards are phrased in an academic manner that shortlists findings and theory from literature on educational administration and management. The tone is also quite paternalistic, and perhaps a bit banal. For instance:

> Good relationships underpin effective leadership. Headship is interpersonal. Headteachers work with and through other people.... To help build positive relationships it is important headteachers understand themselves and the impact they have on others.
>
> (NCSL 2003: 3)

> Headteachers are accountable to themselves and to others. They are accountable for ensuring that pupils enjoy and benefit from high quality education; for promoting the concept of collective responsibility so all stakeholders accept their own accountability; and for contributing to the continued transformation of the education service.
>
> (NCSL 2003: 5)

Headteachers, between law-based reform and these standards, find themselves in a somewhat difficult situation. One way of looking at this situation is positive: it leaves the actual characteristics of headship open, wide, and inclusive. The hidden agenda draws a picture of an endless list of models, types, and styles of running a school. It hints that leadership is diverse and can appear in many shapes and forms. But another way to look at this situation is less optimistic. Leadership is not receiving the same attention that other issues receive. Government does not invest enough in formalisation of headteacher responsibilities and duties.

Another important specific change in the story of headship and law-based reform is the appearance of governing bodies. These are not unique to England's school system. What is quite unique to England, however, is the strong establishment of these bodies through primary legislation that states in an unequivocal manner that 'subject to any other statutory provision, the conduct of a maintained school shall be under the direction of the school's governing body' (EA 2002, part 3, chapter 1, 21). These strong words create a distinct framework of authority for school head-teachers. Or do they? According to research on governing bodies (Earley 2000; Earley and Creese 2003) the reality in schools is a far cry from the words of the law. In accountability terms, the governing bodies have a lot of responsibility and authority but a far from adequate capacity to undertake their duties. They do not understand the material of education enough to take real charge of schools. Headteachers, whom they are supposed to supervise, actually have to coach them constantly – an evident conflict of interest. It seems there are simply not enough suitable governors for 35,000 schools in Britain. The school governing mechanism is a divider between socio-economically strong and weak areas: while stronger schools are able to recruit highly educated governors, who often hold management positions in other organisations in their private professional life, in weak areas the picture is quite different. Strong schools have governors who can afford extensive consulting that assists them in reaching decisions, and can also help the school in acquiring funds and resources. Therefore, the picture depicted by the law is substantially different from the reality of governing bodies in English schools. Fear of negligence lawsuits and lack of compensation for the time required for doing one's job as a governor properly already appear and take their toll.

One ray of light in this dim scene is the relatively recent policy on Performance Management and Threshold Assessment. This set of statutory tools indeed gives headteachers significant new powers. But there are some problems. For instance, Performance Management is not in primary law but in secondary[1] legislation. Also, the procedure is quite complicated and requires significant supervision, first by an external advisor and second, by the governing body's specially appointed members. But this is certainly a step in empowering headteachers in the important field of staff management, and an attempt to equip them with capacity tools that are necessary for carrying out their newly acquired responsibilities.

English law-based reform and accountability mechanisms

Two models were used to analyse educational law. The first is the already classic model by Jacob Adams, from Vanderbilt University in Tennessee, and Michael Kirst from Stanford University in California. Principal-agent theory is at the base of their work. The second model is by Ron Glatter from the UK Open University. Adams and Kirst explain that for accountability systems to work, the accounts – who is accountable to whom, who is the principal, who is the agent – have to be defined. 'The question refers to a relationship in which one party, the principal, engages another party, the agent, to produce outcomes desired by the principal' (Adams and Kirst 1999: 474). Their model identified six domains of accountability and connected them to educational leadership. It emerged from the growing tendency of state legislatures[2] in the United States to enact and implement law-based reform in many areas of educational policy. These reforms include, as in England, a sometimes contradictory mixture of decentralisation and centralisation, regulation and free market policies. The first domain (1999: 467–72) is bureaucratic accountability: ministry and municipality rules and regulations and school supervision. The second domain is legal accountability: fiduciary or contractual obligations embedded in legislation and high court precedents, and constitutional and administrative legislation that establish mandatory accountability in all sorts of areas. The third domain is professional accountability; based on expert knowledge gathered through studies in academic institutions and certified. The fourth domain is political accountability: compliance to demands of constituencies, local government, governing bodies, PTAs, and such. The fifth domain is moral accountability: educational leaders' personal moral codes. Finally, the sixth domain is market accountability, requiring school leaders to respond to market demands, competing with other schools, open enrolment policies, etc. Adams and Kirst explain that understanding the way these types of accountability function is crucial for the chances of law-based reform to succeed in its missions:

> Strengths and weaknesses of any system will manifest to the extent that the match between system and task makes sense ... incompatible design elements, stitched together, reduce accountability's effectiveness ... the balance of responsibilities between principals and agents, and the degree to which principal-agent actions are mutually reinforcing, constitute another factor in system success.
>
> (Adams and Kirst 1999: 473)

Analysis of law-based reform at the end of the Conservative era and subsequently under the Labour government shows some confusion between these types of accountability. Obviously the legal domain has grown much more evident in the life of schools during the past fifteen years or so. But so has the bureaucratic domain. Somewhat contradictory is the fact that the regulatory role of government promotes an agenda of free market and political accountability that require, according to Adams and Kirst, a large degree of freedom for agents (headteachers). A lot of educational law is over-regulated, therefore not exactly allowing agents any freedom. However, the biggest problem with accountability mechanisms is that they are all founded on the idea that a combination of regulation and free market competition will somehow eventually influence teacher–pupil interaction and teaching–learning practices. This means that law-based reform is targeted at lessening the provider-dominated characteristic of public education systems as described by Bottery (2000). So far, this is just an assumption, yet to be proved. Like many other policy initiatives, law-based reform pushes on forward as if this questionable assumption were already a fact. This is the power of managerialist ideology. In Stephen Ball's words, 'Management is a powerful tool of exclusion. Through the application of management techniques, problems or issues, which may have value or ideological aspects, can be translated into technical matters and thus depoliticized' (Ball 1987: 138).

The logic that whole system mandatory policies (legal/bureaucratic accountability) can influence beliefs and perceptions (professional/moral accountability) and then finally behaviour (market/political accountability) is serendipitous, at best. Adams and Kirst do caution that accountability systems that focus on agent behaviour (and tend to lean on rules and regulations) rather than accountability systems that lean on agent capacity, are less likely to achieve their goals. The idea of legal and bureaucratic systems is, that if goals are defined accurately and promoted by tough regulatory tools, coupled with public name and shame systems, then agents will, somehow, change their practices for the better and find within themselves new powers to transform their ways and the ways of their followers (i.e. school staff). This is a myth, of course, and if capacity-building and capacity tools do not accompany the regulation procedure, it will not accomplish what it set out to do. Some necessary conditions are agent's clear expectations, direct causality between actions and their results, certain knowledge concerning the results of agent's actions, adequate resources, and enough discretion (Adams and Kirst 1999: 478). There is enough research that backs up this statement, from the UK (Ouston *et al.* 1998; Radnor *et al.* 1998; Woods 2000) and other countries as well (Cibulka 1999; Cibulka and Derlin 1998; Davis and Gold 2002; Ginsberg and Berry 1998; Wong and Anagnostopoulos 1998). Woods (2000) expresses his worries that instrumental, high stakes characteristics of English law-based reform encourage 'survival tactics' and preference of students from well-to-do families. This is the malady of linear policy planning, that is based on human and social engineering philosophy (Ball 1987; Bottery 1992; Hannaway 2004). The ideas look great on paper, but backfire when implemented. Goldring and Greenfield (2002: 9) refer to this phenomenon as 'hybrid government expectations'.

The second model used for analysing educational law was developed by Ron Glatter (2002: 229, 2003), who identified four domains of accountability, autonomy, and governance. The first domain is Competitive Market (CM): schools are run like a small business, in a voucher-type environment. The second domain is School Empowerment (SE): individual schools are the centre of reform receiving pedagogical and financial autonomy. The third domain is Local Empowerment (LE): autonomy is granted to communities or municipalities – the LEA is the focus of decentralisation. Finally, the fourth model is Quality Control (QC): mandatory curriculum and frequent assessment shape the school as an 'end production point'. The differences between these four models are, according to Glatter, substantial and distinctive. However, an analysis of English educational law shows that it has failed to grasp these discrepancies and hops from one model to the other, quite haphazardly. For instance, after studying the 1998 School Standards and Framework Act, and the 2002 Educational Act, coupled with the 1988 Education Reform Act under the Conservatives, the 1993 and 1996 Education Acts, and the 1996 School Inspections Act, one can conclude that they do not have any of Glatter's models placed as a clear policy target. The Conservative legislation promotes both the CM model (through open enrolment policy) and the SE model (through grant-maintained schools and 'opting out' opportunities). Labour law-based policy strengthens the QC model (through OFSTED – a Conservative institution from 1993 with additional powers from 1998 and 2000, PANDAs, and 'Results' sections on websites and in the *Times Educational Supplement*, etc.). Recent legislation, especially the 2002 Education Act, that added authority to governing bodies is somewhere in between the SE model, because it does strengthen schools, and the LE model, because it passes on authority *from the LEA to the local community and the school.* Performance management policy is definitely inclined to the SE model, as it changes, quite dramatically, headteachers' control over their staff. This mixture of models is not just an academic clash between theory and research. Finally, the *Education Action Zone Handbook* (DfEE 1998), a legal document based on the 1998 School Standards and Framework Act, is a total accountability 'salad bowl' system. It disempowers LEAs, passing on authority to the zone management. It brings in private funds. It disempowers headteachers through the zone control and strengthens them with additional important funds and initiatives. Although it establishes a forum in which all parties have a say, power is in the hands of external directors. This scene is a sobering example of how linear and positivistic thinking control law-based reform, and how the system is wrongly viewed as an orderly set of separate variables that can be contained, isolated, and controlled. The cultural and political reality of schools is quite the opposite, of course. It is more like a mosaic, a maze, or a quilt, of inseparable interdependent and entwined phenomena (even the term 'variable' is inappropriate, for it hints towards positivism), that must be viewed and managed holistically. Glatter, like Adams and Kirst, Woods, and others, is sceptical as to how law-based reform actually reaches its goals. He agrees that headteachers have adopted new leadership skills, but they have also adopted managerial ideologies that may clash with egalitarianism and fairness – two important traits of educational systems in democracies. He states that findings on the change in teaching–learning practices are 'extremely thin' (Glatter 2002: 232) – findings supported by Levacic (2002) and somewhat contradicted by Caldwell (2000, 2002) and Harris (2004). According to Levacic, who has done breakthrough work on both school-based management (Levacic 1995) and economics of education and their link to school-based management (Levacic 2002; Levacic and Woods 2000; Levacic *et al.* 2003):

> One has to be very careful in assessing the vast amount of research on these questions … with these caveats I would conclude that self-managed schools can raise productive standards and that means-tested voucher schemes, if carefully designed, can enhance access to better quality schools for low-income children, though it may not do so for the most deprived. If educational policy-makers are not so concerned with either the productive efficiency of the national school system or with equality of opportunity, then greater school autonomy in a competitive environment promotes allocative efficiency in areas where the private sector has sufficient incentives to respond to market demand. All the efficiency arguments in favour of school autonomy, in either its regulated or competitive form, depend crucially on the capacity of schools to manage their resources efficiently to achieve their educational objectives.
>
> (Levacic 2002: 202)

So facing these thin or, at best, controversial results, it boils down to school leadership and effective management – as Levacic points out.

Analysis of issues of the *Times Educational Supplement* (TES) validates these findings further. One advert for leadership studies shows a man and two women pulling a rope. The text says: 'Do you know how your leadership style impacts on your school?' (TES 13 September 2002: 14). Another headline gives an extreme example of informing parents on educational data: 'Parents get weekly text-message reports … Box Hill School already has a website giving parents access to pupils' records … now they will be able to check on their children and make sure they are getting money's worth' (TES 15 June 2002: 4).

Wood's (2000) concern that accountability systems push headteachers to policies that will boost their school's results, simply by segregation, is strengthened by the following headline: 'Specialist schools are recruiting an increasingly privileged number of students, with church schools among the worst offenders, new research shows' (TES 15 June 2001: 2).

The problems of handling governing bodies are mentioned as well: 'Why is vital information about how well schools are doing being withheld from governors?' (TES 13 September 2002: 32); 'Governors despite their legal duty to promote high standards of education … are being cut out of a vital information loop' (TES 13 September 2002: 32).

Then again, as accountability models mix and clash, the following headlines appeared on headteacher autonomy in the light of standards and school inspections: 'In practice, more autonomy for schools usually means more autonomy for head-teachers' (TES 13 September 2002: 32); 'John Dunford, general secretary of the Secondary Heads Association, said: "We have to reduce reliance on external exams and bring in more rigorous internal assessment."' (TES 15 June 2001: 3); 'Schools had forged good relationships with education department staff, but inspectors warned: this has also led to a familiarity within which communication is not always as sharp as it might be' (TES 15 June 2001: 20).

Meanwhile the teacher workforce is anxious when new policies increase their workload with no increase in wages: 'The National Association of Schoolmasters Union of Women Teachers has advised members to refuse to mark the optional maths and English test papers to prevent increases in workload' (TES 15 June 2001: 18); 'The assembly has pledged to "free up teachers' time to teach, by reducing the burden of paperwork", and education minister Jane Davidson is committed to ending multiple requests from different bodies for the same information' (TES 15 June 2001: 18).

Some headlines show the ambiguousness of law-based reform that navigates between empowering schools, empowering LEAs, and involving global companies in urban renewal: 'Do we need a commercial break? Campaigners call for tighter controls as schools become increasingly reliant on cash from big business' (TES 13 September 2002: 26); 'Inspectors have praised three education authorities for building up a good relationship with their schools and for their strong leadership' (TES 28 September 2002: 10); 'She [Morris] expects there will be more differentiation between schools: much greater freedom for the successful and continued close scrutiny and support for the struggling' (TES 15 June 2001: 5).

The following headlines indicate the growing concern of heads regarding the link between policy and their own capabilities to take on the challenges of current headship: 'We deserve bigger rise than our staff, say heads. Managers demand "clear blue water" between their salaries and those of senior class teachers' (TES 13 September 2002: 4); '"Old-fashioned" management structures are blamed for upping teacher absence rate' (TES 5 October 2001: 3); 'Most head-teachers say they went into the job barely prepared for the challenges with one in 10 feeling "frightened" by the responsibility' (TES 13 September 2002: 7); ' … were particularly concerned about the lack of commitment on the part of schools to the plan, the main vehicle to pushing through improvement, warning that Heads were unclear about its status' (TES 15 June 2001: 20).

The conclusion of this chapter is that law-based reform should bear much more in mind headteachers, school management, and school leadership, and not take for granted these important factors of success as natural by-products of legislation, regulation, and mandatory accountability schemes. The following three chapters offer evidence of this assumption among English school headteachers.

3 Strong laws – strong schools: how entrepreneur headteachers advance their schools under law-based reform

This chapter presents the stories[1] of four headteachers who represent strong schools in well-to-do areas. One is a big city comprehensive. Two are suburban comprehensive high schools. One is a grammar school. The schools presented here are schools that 'seize the day' and take advantage of the quasi-market situation that characterises law-based reform under the Labour government. In many ways they actually flourish – they and their headteachers.

Case 1[2] From school to college: making use of law's opportunities in a global context

Anthony's school is situated between two neighbourhoods: an affluent area, where many popular media and art figures reside, and a council estate – an area of public housing inhabited by poor, recently arrived Asian immigrants, some of them illegally in Britain. Several large elegant red-brick buildings welcome the newcomer, including a separate building for the sixth form, an indoor swimming pool, and a laboratory and science building. Anthony, the head, in his forties, has a BSc and an MBA. He is a veteran in this school, having served as deputy head for several years before achieving principalship. On the role of law in his work, he states the following:

> Law certainly focuses the mind and it very quickly gets the whole school going when you know that government initiative has been law-based since 1988, legislation being used as a policy tool, and we are very well used to the Secretary of State using this power to change policy. In many ways in our school, people get to accept that, while in

the past, they tried to subvert it. Now they try to shape it. There's much less resistance, and should the intention if not the letter be followed, we can still progress. We have a board of legislation that is convenient to ignore things that are not in the best interest of the school.

Anthony's school is currently under law-based reform siege that puts constraints on him and on his staff, but also provides great opportunities. The council has created sixth-form schools, also known as 16–19 colleges. These are specially built schools to increase the numbers of students obtaining five A–C GCSEs, which are needed when applying for a place at university. Such schools offer the cream of the comprehensive schools' students better teachers and better learning environments. But these new schools pose a threat to schools like Anthony's: not only do they remove the leading age group from the school, but often also high quality teachers, who lead subject teams, carry responsibilities as senior and middle management team members, and have experience in preparing students for GCSEs and A level exams. The older students have an important 'regulating' effect on younger students, as seniors, perhaps, have elsewhere in the world. However, it is not automatic that sixthformers go on to the new college: the comprehensive schools are allowed to keep their students if their numbers do not fall below a certain number, below which a proper level of educational service cannot be provided. The new sixth-form college is therefore an incentive for improvement. Anthony's reaction has been to upgrade his school into a City Technology College (CTC). These schools, which were introduced by the Conservative government and then promoted under Labour, although there were not more than a couple of dozen by 2000, offer advanced ICT and science education. They also have greater flexibility in offering new school-based programmes, and are allowed freedom in searching for external funds. Anthony and his team spotted a local educational 'market' among Muslim Asian immigrants who live on the council estates that are part of the school's catchment area. The school had good facilities that were not in use in the evenings. The Muslim families include women who stay at home and have problems leaving home for long hours, especially in the evenings, to study in academic institutions that are not in the vicinity, and their culture makes it difficult for them to work outside the home. So the school began offering ICT evening courses. These began on a small scale and evolved into a mini-college that liaises with a university to give academic credit to the students. Not only do these courses allow the women to receive higher education, but computer skills allow certain types of home-based work, which fits in with the traditional Muslim family life. The new programme tempts the sixth-form teachers to stay in the school and upgrades their salaries too. Anthony feels educational law has been important in introducing this change through new mechanisms of accountability, which change his role, though not always towards a clearer one:

> The accountability is huge in terms of who you are accountable to, you know we have a budget of £5 million and the well-being of young people, so I'm accountable to parents, governing bodies, LEA, countless government agencies. My immediate boss? Well, you see I'm hesitating – sometimes I talk to myself. I guess I have to be accountable to the governors but I have to say the relationship we have with the LEA is a real partnership. Although we have to write reports, it doesn't feel like a top-down heavy.

Educational law leaves Anthony puzzled as to who is really responsible for the school and its policy. He is aware that these new mechanisms, including OFSTED inspections and placing schools under 'special measures', have substantial impact, but he is sceptical about whether these changes actually improve failing schools:

> My school inspector comes and works alongside. They have to be responsive to the needs of the schools with public–private partnerships. They discuss with you. We are lucky. But some schools that are not doing so well may feel the LEA is more heavy-handed and not so supportive. I think the move to OFSTED inspection had a huge impact on how we operate. The standardisation, lesson observations, really having to use data on students' prior knowledge: without OFSTED this would not have been embedded in the culture of the schools. There is far greater confidence that sharing good practice in a school is much more common – high-level professional dialogue, and this is a result of the four-year OFSTED cycle. There was huge fear and resistance about

this kind of approach and now it's quite normal and this is quite healthy, though the process is diabolically awful and a huge waste of school resources. But I have to say, schools have changed for the better but there are better ways of doing this. Where you see the negative impact is where schools are failing again and again and I don't believe in getting this identified in the public domain and I hardly see any schools getting out of this, including fresh start which is not successful either. Maybe I'm naive or more community oriented, but I think the way it works with LEAs can work with schools too. Because OFSTED inspection allows someone who knows nothing of the school to understand what's going on. This wouldn't happen if LEAs did it and you would have an ongoing process.

Anthony is aware, though, that there are vast differences among LEAs and their capability to monitor and improve schools. Some are too poor. Others are corrupt or so politicised that the people who run them are quite biased and tend to favour some schools and not others: 'This government is about breaking this Serbian structure of corruption in many LEAs.'

Anthony explains that educational law does indeed shape many parts of school life:

Long term, long history child protection legislation, we stick to these absolutely although like all legislation that involves people they are flawed, they are designed to protect children, and the adults that work with them. We want to be creative, but new staff are shocked on how structured this is and it's a comfort to have this backup. The legislation is in a way something that has tremendous support, but many staff don't know this and maybe this is a good thing, but legislation is not something to be aware of by staff but much more by senior management and by myself.

As a comprehensive school that has achieved CTC status, Anthony's school enjoys the best of both worlds:

It's not like a g-m [grant-maintained] school where you might have to cover yourself all the time. Admissions policy, we work with the LEA, it's one area where parents try to break the law by falsifying information and bribery which are cultural issues. The desperation from parents, we have 210 places in each year group. If you have to have special needs you can get a place here. You have social and medical criteria but this is never ever used. Siblings have automatic right, and nearness to school as the crow flies. Several schools in X claim to be comprehensive but select on basis of music or religion. So people may see us as a neighbourhood school but are not within a mile and they find it difficult to understand that they pay taxes to the council and people from X get their way in. The LEA is very thorough.

The current situation allows schools to decide in what business they are. The once shiny possibility to 'opt out', so appealing in the early 1990s, is not as appealing any more. This is because grant-maintained schools (now called foundation schools) are forced to trade the relative security of LEA backing and maintenance for financial independence. Sometimes this is a good deal, but when the school needs a large sum of money to renovate, the LEA deal may be a lot better. In Anthony's school, both deals exist at the same time. However, Anthony points to the gap between legal requirements and capacity tools:

A much better move towards leadership teams and headship teams, there was the head figure and worker bees. In progressive schools, you are far less likely to make mistakes but some people would think you are more cautious. In middle management, legislation has a lot of impact in target setting and having the department ready for threshold and performance management. So professional possibilities are much more evident than they were before. I think we have a thin flat middle management tier and we need to look at clustering. Also having this thin flat model can prevent movement to a more senior position. People, they are certainly much more aware than they were. They are always torn apart and now have the responsibility of senior manager too. This structure has to be looked at, I don't feel the differential is looked at. My head of science is teaching as much as the rest and managing a budget and all of this for a few thousand quid more. We haven't seen how extensive it is: we all teach on the management team. They pay a lot to these people to teach. It's getting the balance right. In industry, it's acknowledged that a manager's role is different. Education management is about people – if you teach all the time how can you manage them? I have a friend who is a city consultant and he has very little budget control. And he is paid as a leading medical professional, while my head of science gives out rooms. That's what the advanced skills teachers were to do. We don't have any here.

In more than one way, Anthony's school represents the better side of English law-based reform in the early twenty-first century. Although it has some problems dealing with the stress that has been forced down upon it in a very short period, it is coping well with the situation. This is an example of success through educational legislation. The school uses the framework provided by the law, a framework of a quasi-market within (mostly) public funds, to expand its horizons, areas of interest, educational goals, and consumer groups. Meanwhile, it resists the attempt to fragment the system through the new sixth-form college and simultaneously improves the range and quality of the programmes offered to its traditional public. All along, it succeeds in keeping a truly comprehensive environment, bringing change to a run-down poor council estate and retaining the majority of its affluent 'constituency', which is so necessary for its academic and financial survival. Anthony's leadership is one that looks beyond school boundaries and sees educational law-based reform with professional and far-seeing eyes. The school is lucky to have him, at this time.

Case 2 'Policy has its bits in bold, so I'm told': social policy in an affluent school

Sally is the headteacher of a large countryside comprehensive high school, situated among affluent villages and a small town. An impressive set of modern, clean-cut buildings welcome the newcomer to Sally's school. A large 'learning centre' is situated at the heart of the main building, offering a variety of possibilities for the students. These include multimedia technology, books, ICT of all kinds – all organised into cosy corners and small amphitheatres, with new wall-to-wall carpeting in an air-conditioned enclave. This learning centre has been financed by a trust fund set up by parents. Before becoming the headteacher of this school, Sally was the headteacher of an inner city primary school in a tough area, renowned as a crime-ridden, drug-infested neighbourhood.

> When you say law, a chunk of the things that come to mind is health and safety. And after that it's the statutory around National Curriculum, SEN, staffing, threshold assessment, parents' rights, exclusion and the other side is litigation. I'm increasingly conscious of the statutory relations with LEA. There's the financial issue like audit openness and transparency, my relationship with the governors, my delegated responsibility and the policies we're required to have. And some of that will be constraining and some is clarifying and then there are implications of management, social exclusions and pupil support. The union. So it's all the levels, DfEE to LEA, LEA to governors and the stakeholders: unions, pupils, and parents.

Sally emphasises that schools in tough neighbourhoods are often not only poor in resources but also suffer from poor management, which makes things worse, and poorly run councils: 'My context is different because when I was headteacher in X and it was run very badly, we weren't a GM school but we opted out.' The 1988 ERA allowed schools to 'opt out' formally and receive 'grant-maintained' (now foundation) status. But quite a few headteachers report that many schools 'opt out' informally and move forward (not necessarily progressively) to school-based type management. Educational law has gradually become an important part of Sally's work and professional life.

Exclusions and permanent exclusions are a serious issue in English law-based reform, one that is a source of endless frustration among headteachers:

> You have to know those legal systems to be able to play them. I've never abused exclusion and I think I never did. We are an inclusive school. There were heads that abused the system, so we don't use indefinite or permanent exclusion. I have said to a parent today: 'I'll have to consider it and I'm not allowed to say this but is this the right place for your son?'

This egalitarian approach is typical of the views that headteachers like Sally and Anthony hold and express. It is typical of all headteachers in this study, who run schools in well-to-do areas. It is a powerful statement. In Sally's school, extra money from an affluent LEA, plus a trust fund set up by parents, offer assistance on this issue. Sally sees pupil retention as an indicator of the school's as well as her personal–professional success. As the school is in an upper middle-class area, the number of pupils facing permanent exclusion is relatively low, certainly when compared to inner city schools as presented in Chapter 4:

> We said it's on the cards. Do you jump or do I push. It's wrong but I don't have enough support teachers to do intervention work. I have one afternoon a week per pupil on behaviour management and that's not enough. The process of reinstatement is so long; while the government wants to lower the number of reinstated students, it's the same on attendance and reducing exclusion. Social inclusion and pupil support are good because it's a guideline and it's not personal anymore. It protects us, it's nice to tuck behind that. My annual return in year 11 includes my exclusions. I get a lot of money for these kids in pupil retention grants, so I bought a teacher with that and this penalty is useful, but it doesn't impact on my decision. The government makes us think again but this is for financial reasons not educational reasons. When I worked before I came here, they had a Catholic school with 180 pupils in September and 120 in the OFSTED exam so they excommunicated 60.... Schools lie, cheat and massage figures. Some schools say, 'if you don't wear the uniform you don't come back'. But my view is that learning is more important but I can't say that. So if I exclude this child it will be a negative statistic. So the law and league tables are constraints on my work.

Sally refers to a policy that puts a cap on school exclusions but also backs it with finance for 'behaviour management'. The money is generally not enough, but in Sally's school in which there is a relatively small number of exclusion-prone pupils together with surplus funds from the LEA and a parents' trust fund, the situation is satisfactory.

This brings Sally to talk about accountability, and how educational law shapes the surroundings of the school, and its interdependencies with the forces represented by parents, local authorities, national authorities, etc.

I should be accountable to students and parents.... The governors are parents, they reflect parents' views. The LEA is the whipping boy. The government is passionate about education, but I'm kind of fed up of this rhetoric and the idea that we are not. I try to express this to staff because staff are not good at handling complaints. Those interpersonal skills teachers have had to learn. I see myself *with* the governors in coalition against the LEA. We always look for someone to blame or to be the big bad wolf. It's always somebody else's fault, so I don't tend to work the governors against the premises but my governors are people I'd work with. But if they are critical of my staff I go back to the staff. Parents are still, when they criticise or have a concern, not able to voice their concern on equal levels although this is a communication society, and I get many things on e-mail. But Bengali parents don't have Toshibas. As for the DfEE, it's simply too far away. Their main influence is through the law.

So, although educational law says a lot about the structure of the system and the division of authority, responsibility, and accountability, the situation is far from clear. Sally is a headteacher with a wide viewpoint, because this is her second post as head and her academic background is on educational policy. And even she finds drawing an exact map of power and hierarchy problematic, at best. An important factor in the map of power is the government-administered testing and audit:

The league tables came out today. They don't tell about individuals and their story. I suppose if I could, I would like to say rude things about OFSTED. By creating the accountability, it has done something, but I know schools who get only good students. If my little lad who doesn't speak English gets a 'B', it's a big thing but it doesn't show on the tables. We've had OFSTED in 97 and I'd rather have OFSTED walk in tomorrow unannounced because you can scrub for OFSTED, you can sit day and night and prepare the paperwork.

League tables and OFSTED inspections become a linchpin in law-based reform for headteachers like Sally. Not knowing whom they are accountable to, they are quite clear about the role of audit in governing their work, role, and school. In the absence of clear definitions on the hierarchy, inspections become a type of hierarchy themselves. Sally connects this with the mechanism of performance management, a relatively new mechanism designed to allow headteachers control over teachers' pay, as an incentive to improve results in several areas of their work, including curriculum and programme development, achievement on tests, and so on:

> Performance management is a new thing, I'm being told that policy has 'bits in bold' we cannot change. It's the kind of idea that they give you control and there is much more accountability in schools. You wanted it so you take it. I was head of English when National Curriculum came in and I had a baby and I was on maternity leave and we were involved in GCSEs and it was a straitjacket and we asked what are we going to do about that and everyone looked at me like I was mad because it was a fait accompli so there was nothing to fight and it's now how many years from there? And there is a policy with bits that are not negotiable. It's the idea of saying one thing and doing another. We're against performance and pay but we can't come from there. We are not motivated by money. I said I'd like more time and teachers. I like more money for my weekend but I like weekends. I'd like more hours for my teachers, if it comes in the form of £2,000 for threshold performance for a teacher. Here's a head who is passionate about children and can quote the government better than they can, so let me do the job.

Sally welcomes the latest reforms, but cautions that they create dangerously large workloads for underpaid staff. Here the headteacher's organisational and moral, or political, role in getting it all together becomes critical. Sally summed up her agenda in a long monologue. I sat there fascinated and just tried to get it all down on my laptop:

> We create an understanding that there is a solution but the service is underfunded and we create an expectation that cannot be fulfilled. I try to be there on the drop of the hat and spin on it. The 1988 [ERA] became a dictatorship so we subvert it. We want to do something not because it's different, but because it's an entitlement. This school delivers the National Curriculum. It's a foundation, on which we build our own curriculum. Every child has two hours of drama a week and having said that, the new National Curriculum is a reasonable and readable

document looking on citizenship – why do they look at that? Because they want children to vote in four and eight years. That's what I think it's about. I welcome a national curriculum about sex education and drug abuse; there should be national programme on that. In my previous school, I would welcome something like that, if I was at age 5 in X [a tough rural area]. If I were in X [posh neighbourhood where Anthony's school is] at age 11 I wouldn't miss anything. Blair talks on combined initiatives. What the government is trying to do, the zeal comes from the top, and you have to wind up people better so people won't just quote the government. You have to win the schools to your argument and not impose on them. The Left made the mistake for not claiming excellence, and being uncomfortable with it, they left it to the Right. We should reclaim that and then not be grumpy about league tables. I'm having our school under review on performance indicators as well as basic information, but on my list, I want to show who are on school plays, who take part in assemblies. We should reclaim those things so that we can say, 'here is my evidence'. I did my dissertation on pupils' voice. I talked to heads who said, 'I'm right, but I cannot present the data about it'. I had some tell me: 'we had less damage this year, and I thought what if we had the evidence base that we didn't have'. We wrote a prospectus in my other school and there was a real change in school culture, how we as heads are required to be. Some heads say: 'I have 78 staff and I say I have 1800' – pupils included – so it takes the shape of what the government says. These are examples of best practice. The Green Papers, the SEN things. They are trying to listen. Roland Barth says that the clever government is that which helps you retain your individuality. It's a bit like the football and the manager. There's a football manager's role about headship.

Sally voices uneasiness about how law-based reform actually shapes her world. Between the lines there is admiration for the government's remarkable capability and success in creating substantial change in a system that used to be heavily 'producer-dominated' (Harris 1993: 245), and is now government-regulated and consumer-controlled. But her professional pride is a bit hurt. After all, if the government speaks about school autonomy and local management, should the Ministry practise a better sense of partnership than the 'top-down' approach? The 'forked tongue' of government is quite puzzling.

Case 3 Away from it all: Valerie's country retreat from paperwork

Valerie's school is a grammar-turned-comprehensive. Set in the middle of an endless green meadow with many trees and flowers, the one-storey spread-out campus reminded me of American suburban schools. The campus is quite spacious, the buildings are uniform: brown stone, red, tiled roofs. Entering the administrative area, I noticed a commotion which turned out to be prospective parents and their children, dressed up, arriving for enrolment interviews. This is a very well-to-do area, large private homes, or perhaps estates, welcoming to the visitor. A small remembrance monument is situated in the midst of the busy corridor that leads to the headteacher's office. The monument pays homage to school graduates killed in the Second World War. It also shows some of the somewhat aristocratic past of this school. Not that it lacks aristocracy now, but it is different: modern, self-confident, and aware of current social and political trends. Valerie, the headteacher, is just attempting to get through the paperwork of Performance Management regulations. Her desk is practically covered with reports, of several kinds, and she says she puts in extra hours every night attempting to have them done according to schedule:

> Obviously being in a politicised profession like teaching means being servants of the political people and their whims. I suppose the most important is Performance Management. There is a great centralisation force and there is lack of joined-up thinking and there is a rush to get things through. It seems completely unprofessional and there is a lack of consultation that had brought some of my colleagues to tears. Headteachers have to set targets with an external advisor, but there aren't any, so they keep setting a new deadline and the law is losing face. The principles are good, but the implementation is very difficult. I have a staff of over 100 and I'm accountable to them and we keep receiving egg on our face.

Valerie has some thoughts on decentralisation and the systems structure:

> Also, there are no clear ideas on the role of local government. There is
> a lot of duplication. We receive things from the DfEE and then the same
> from the LEA a few weeks later. They are fighting for their life and for
> keeping their jobs. Other heads told me I'm not compelled by law to
> give them this information. I had just received a 48-page form on
> curriculum planning and of course we have this, but it's such a waste of
> time so I didn't do it and we are a group of heads who got organised on
> this.

The feeling one gets from Valerie is that of intense pressure to comply
with various regulations without which she would receive much fewer
opportunities for her students than she has now:

> We also bid on everything to get something – we have a number of
> projects done together. Because of this system, we are building a class
> building and a food technology hall and trying to teach at the same
> time. The balance between being accountable and working within the
> law and producing the paper is really tough. One issue is permanent
> exclusion. We do that quite rarely. I've gone through the new guidelines
> and they are so complex that you don't exclude, which I suppose is the
> target of the government. I spent 15 hours filling the forms and 14
> appendices. And it will be appealed. Being a free aid school we are
> oversubscribed and we get 50 appeals from parents and we had this for
> several years and it's OK, but now we had four cases coming to the
> ombudsman and most of my work goes on these things. I don't have a
> proper support system. Our personnel department people are
> continuously engaged and their phone is always busy. We just started
> taking money from parents. This has been our first financial year on
> LEA budget and we had a deficit and launched the anchor fund and we
> have trustees and we want to get money in and distribute it to
> the departments for books and paper for the photocopier. We have
> a language college being built with some sponsorship. We received
> £117,000 from the DfEE but the rest is sponsored by various
> agencies.

Indeed, outside an ultramodern building is being put up, skylight and all. This will soon be the new language centre. The ability to get more money for the school is a relatively new option for community schools. It offers great opportunities to schools like this one but of course widens gaps between schools from poor and affluent areas and might tempt authorities to adopt more 'budget neutral' policies. On the other hand, it allows community (LEA) and foundation schools to top up their budget and compete with voluntary aided schools.

Law-based reform seems to Valerie an endless list of demands, most of them bureaucratic in nature.

> They are trying to drive up standards and it's good but there's no appreciation of the head's work. It's an issue for governing bodies of schools. Laypeople come in and discuss educational issues. They are all volunteers and they say we have more and more responsibilities and the onus is on me to deal with their day-to-day work. It took six inches of documents telling them about this, and these people are determining my pay. I looked around the room and saw an IT person, a nurse, a primary schoolteacher and a retired Marks & Spencer salesman. Between having a 'critical friend' and educating these friends so they can do their job – it has gone out of hand. There isn't any other profession that has laypeople advising and actually running the school. I get along fine with them but I hate to think what's it like if it isn't this way – it must be a nightmare. The policy is implemented but at what cost? You can't do other things.

Valerie is attempting to keep a balance between her work as a coalition builder and maintaining the necessary external alliances, and building a complex infrastructure that can run the school properly, far from external pressures:

> We had to move to a leadership team scenario, which I have serious misgivings about what we should have. We are four: myself, two deputies and one assistant who is actually a more poorly paid head … so each one has his own responsibility: curriculum planning, evaluation, and performance management and we have an excellent management team that receive five responsibility points. One is responsible for

pastoral care, another for outside agencies. I didn't see a team of seven meeting continually. So we meet once a week and we have five people who are advisors to governors' committees. We have meetings of heads of departments and year heads. Dovetailing with that we have people doing things like exams and career officers and SEN co-ordinator who get middle management salaries.

The problem as Valerie explained it, is that running this system is a job in itself. So decentralising the schools and delegating authority, though useful for staff morale and for broadening staffs' horizons, also adds another permanent workload on the headteacher. Therefore, Valerie sees the new laws as a mixed blessing:

The advent of the National Curriculum and the data around it are actually sophisticated and accountability systems are much better than they used to be. We used to do things very subjectively. We said 'he is a good teacher' but we didn't know why. We had heads of department analyse their A level work. Now they have better data to go on. There is more access to higher education and students can go to university and have a £15,000 debt. The PANDA report showed that 95 per cent of our targets are met and students succeed.

Case 4 Young at heart: managing Dave's grammar

For a foreign researcher visiting English schools, entering Dave's grammar school is like visiting the set of a film. All through my visit, I was wondering whether the scenery is real or perhaps these are large cardboard coulisses – parts of a Hollywood studio, and whether somebody was shooting a movie about an 'old boys' school. It is situated in a green scenery of shrubs, narrow paths with high hedges on each side, an ancient medieval church nearby, and an old arched entrance on which the date the school was founded, in the sixteenth century is engraved just by its emblem and French-Latin slogan. This is a boys-only suburban government school.

Dave, the head, is a lively, alert man, not quite the stereotype one may imagine when coming to this school. The slightly casual look – that includes a tweed jacket, a canvas tie, and perhaps a flannel shirt – is definitely *not* Dave, who is wearing a meticulous, dark-blue three-piece business suit. His recent degree, one of several, is a master's in business administration. Despite the old-fashioned air that lingers in his school, there is nothing old-fashioned about Dave's demeanour. He is tough, has a quick response, and sees a bright future ahead. His attitude is managerial, but not ruthless. He is perhaps the best example I found in this study of how law-based reform has shaped headship and leadership cultures in English schools in the past few years. Dave seems to be very well acquainted with recent law-based reform:

> Education law establishes the whole format and procedure as to how the school is run. This is a foundation school. The title 'foundation school' is different from the original title of the school and forms its own original title – grant-maintained. We employ our own staff and we see minimal interference from the LEA. We are accountable in a legal sense to the LEA – they can't sack our staff, but they can sack me … we follow the framework 1998 act and there is little room for manoeuvre.

These words are, concisely, the story of what happened to so many English schools from the 1990s. Dave's was an elitist inclusive boys grammar school, then became an LEA grammar school and then 'opted out' and became a foundation school. These of course are not just titles. They represent a fundamental change in the system and in schools, which happened over a relatively short time and caused considerable upheaval. Head-teachers of such schools were judged in terms of productivity, continuity, stability, and conservatism. There is a sharp contrast between the physical appearance of the school and Dave's views on educational policy and school management.

> One biggest, not law but quasi-legal issue, is that of social inclusion. We've had to radically change many of our practices very quickly. We did not have to consult the LEA on permanent exclusions, but we have to reduce our exclusion rate without further resources and no matter what you think of this, it will be seen as a sign of weakness.

So Dave, who declares that he is a passionate advocate of Labour's law-based reform, is weighing the pros and cons of elitist schooling. His school has a very good reputation in the area, and is immensely over-subscribed. This is important for the school's survival and ongoing development. But inclusion is out – exclusion is in. Dave explains that the government sends a mixed message – encouraging, or at least maintaining, grammar schools, which by definition are not comprehensive – and promoting inclusion policy. Perhaps the answer lies in the inclusion or exclusion mechanism of grammar schools:

> When I arrived we had seven criteria, special needs, sons of old boys, children of staff, siblings who had or have a brother in school (usually who have), this is old grammar school tradition. We had some interesting cases from the ombudsman especially from ethnic minorities. We had to back off. It's gone. We still have children of staff. At some point, it may be challenged and it may go. We have a chosen circle of 27 primary schools and the other schools are mounting an argument that this is disadvantaging. The Secretary of State agreed this list a few years ago. We have to operate on best value and competitive tendering has been around a long time.

Therefore, the school is moving from evident SES-based enrolment, which does not provide for any social mobility, to an attainment-based meritocratic system. This is still exclusive, but quite different from before. Of course, SES and class are still intervening variables but they are not as significant as previously. Using the analogy of the half-filled glass, then, is the glass half empty or half full? The Labour government would point at the full half, of course. Important empirical research like Gillborn and Youdell's (2000) impressive, insightful book *Rationing Education* says the opposite, as does other policy analysis (Whitty *et al.* 1998). Preserving grammar schools and the benefits they receive still happens under law-based reform in England (Levacic *et al.* 2003).

Dave explains how his school manages the centralisation versus decentralisation effects of law-based reform:

> We are constrained by the National Curriculum and its requirements. Governments will decree, and civil servants will enable, but the difficulty is to understand schools and finance them. The Special Needs

Code of Practice was a 'budget neutral' arrangement, which means find the money. Such changes are difficult to sustain. For example, the ICT in every subject is a major strand. It's an aspiration but also a legal requirement. We were ofsteded [OFSTED has become a verb in English 'Headspeak'] and ICT was a key issue. Our staff cost is high, our buildings were built 400 years ago, and we don't get additional funds. We have to replace windows according to English Heritage ways and restoration laws. It puts tremendous pressures on us. We take 180 boys and had 1,000 applicants. There is a brand new school so it's either modern facilities or traditions.

'Budget neutral' is the key phrase in this extract. It means that since English schools have gained financial autonomy; the government is tempted to implement expensive reforms without backing them up with reasonable funding. In the past, in case of every such reform, headteachers could ask for rooms, staff, etc., or else avoid the policy altogether. Now they are asked to 'adjust' and decide by themselves where the money should come from. Up to a certain limit, this is possible, but only just. When expensive mandatory initiatives begin to accumulate, then financial autonomy becomes a slogan, no more. Attempting to keep age-old traditions, including the splendour of a 500-year-old campus – which is not only very expensive to maintain but also impossible to heat and difficult to provide modern services in – is another paradox. Other heads of foundation schools in this study are worried that financial autonomy is a mixed blessing which sometimes restricts their options – despite its original appeal after years of being dependent on LEA financing and support. Time and experience have lessened the appeal of the grant-maintained (now foundation) status. Many community (former LEA) schools now receive near-to-foundation autonomy, without completely losing the backing of the municipal authority. This brings Dave to the issue of staff management, which he and many other headteachers see as the cornerstone of their capability to advance their schools in the free market created by government:

I guess Performance Management is a big issue, I firmly believe in it. It is the most important legal requirement that any government has ever given to a head. I don't subscribe to the view that many heads and teachers claim that education is somehow different from the rest of the world and that rules that do apply to the rest of the world don't apply to us. There is no reason why a teacher should not be held accountable. It allows me to enhance effective teachers and get rid of ineffective teachers. The kids only get through schools once, and I can't tolerate an ineffective staff. I got rid of some through legal means, some foul teachers who think they are not accountable and, end of story, they go. It actually helps a lot by cutting across employment law, and gives us the data. The NUT case presents them in a bad light and most of this was a spin of the NHS in the 1970s. Some staff are here 30 years and although we have normalised things to some extent, some staff remember the grammar school days and so things are comparatively becoming worse, because demands by pupils' parents and the public are quite different now and these old customs are not tolerated anymore. People talk of the good old days but I had a teacher who came in, sat down, read *The Times*, and asked the boys to read in silence. Nowadays there is no hiding place.

Dave is a true CEO of his school and speaks a lot about management and leadership. He thinks modern management is at the heart of running schools in the framework created by the Conservative and then Labour governments in the last fifteen years or so:

The fact is that future heads will have to be trained. The number of heads applying for headship is decreasing and so is the number of heads remaining in their posts. I work 75 hours a week, I'm here at half past six in the morning till seven in the evening and two evenings and many Saturdays in our detention centre. There is a lot of burnout. We didn't work like this five years ago. This is part of how they implement these laws without budget. We simply cover the balance by more and more hours – especially the senior staff and the head. I inherited a large senior management team: five senior teachers and two deputies. Within six months, I completely shaped the senior management more like a commercial management. The school was run as an old-fashioned grammar and the word management was not in use. We are teachers, we have nothing to do with management. Part of my MBA was rubbing shoulders with people from companies like Shell, Glaxo, and Unilever. So here at the school I had everyone have a clear task assigned: this is the pupil and this is the key task. I have a manager for each Key Stage 3, 4, 5 and I don't want to know about it unless it's big, bad, and pear-shaped. If it doesn't have to do with school policy, it's different. They still come in and have a chat, which is OK. But I think managers should manage. I brought the senior administrative person in to the senior management team. We couldn't get someone from the marketplace with this salary. I have managers at all levels wasting their time doing things they shouldn't be doing. I haven't seen any school with an admin staff that is appropriate. We have a one-day a week reprographics person and two word-processing people and any business this size would have six.

Dave points out a serious flaw in government school management policy – not only in England. Government is quick to adopt managerial rhetoric and managerial style human resource management, which means throwing away tenure and other labour rights rather quickly, but is much slower in adopting the administrative standards of real free market business, including proper ICT equipment, legal and financial professional advice, etc. But Dave, like other heads, cannot imagine losing his financial autonomy whatever the circumstances or ramifications:

> I would be happy if the LEA disappeared. Too much money goes to the centre. Since things went back to LEA, we lost £250,000 to central needs. We do help other schools and we may want to sell that some-time. If the LEA wanted something, I'd sell it to them. The LEA won't get new windows unless we give them our money, which we shall not. They are a paper tiger legally accountable for government to school standards but they do not have any influence on that.

This scornful attitude exemplifies the insecure status of LEAs under law-based reform. It is clear that there should be a ministry of education, and the DfES has succeeded in securing its position as a regulator and over-all supervisor of the system. The role of schools is of course quite secure, too, as being the end units that actually provide education in the field. The LEA's role is endlessly disputable and open for debate. Adding governing bodies to schools strengthens them and adds direct public-based authority to the school – an asset reserved so far for the LEA, which, as an elected body, represents the local public that receives schooling.

> I have an exceptionally talented governing body that is just going through radical changes. Five years ago, they had the foresight to have an appointment from outside. Both my deputies applied. The governors were old boys who clearly knew what they wanted. This was the hallmark of the governing body – they are very protective of the school but want it to move forward. They are the best in devotion and backing. The ex-chairman is the vicar who put in enormous time, about a day a week. What we expect in the UK from our governing bodies is enormous. I haven't come across a case of a group of volunteers who have day jobs and on top of it control a three and a half million pound budget, hiring and firing, and are held accountable by the government to every aspect and are receiving a peanut. Some of my governors have business acumen or educational experience. So 19 people sit around a beige table, accept responsibility, and take or support major decisions – it's fine if these people are on the job. It's really OK. I wouldn't be happy if just anyone did that.

Of course, schools like Dave's have the benefit of having a professional governing body that really empowers the school and its head.

Our talk ends with a Dave's 'policy statement' on English law-based reform, a type of educational 'bottom line' that sums up both his criticism and his support for the Labour government's policy. Like several other heads, he takes part in implementing and spreading government policy as an instructor mentor, and lately as an OFSTED inspector:

> In terms of opportunity, I'm very clear that more children have been enfranchised than ever before. In the 1970s, when I was head of science, many children weren't even offered the opportunity of external exams. One of the most wonderful things is the new system of GCSEs, and if a child has acquired the basic work, they will not be denied the opportunity. We only had one or two boys last year that didn't take one exam at least. So many of the reforms have actually changed attitudes. I think league tables have done a lot to raise expectations in all sorts of people's minds. OFSTED has done a tremendous job despite the criticism. I've

been to many schools [as an OFSTED inspector] where at the end of it staff say, 'you have confirmed we are doing a good job and given us points for the future'. But I've never put a school on special measures. I think it's important that OFSTED carries on, but the team of inspectors should be practitioners – teachers or others who are close to the field – the credibility factor is highly important. Sometimes these people have never worked in the public domain, or haven't been in it for fifteen years.

How do schools like Dave's contribute to the implementation of such an egalitarian view? Time will tell.

Conclusion

The schools and heads presented in this chapter may be the types of schools and heads envisioned in the 1990s law-based reforms for England's education system. They are confident, aware of policy, imaginative, and independent. The headteachers have egalitarian views and wish to achieve an egalitarian, fair, and just policy within their schools and their surroundings. These heads are strong supporters of recent law-based reforms with some reservations. Mainly, they want even more autonomy. They think LEAs are redundant. They do not find their place in the new structure. They have managerial ideas and knowledge and want to cut red tape as much as possible. They feel better under Labour policy than under the Conservatives, but there is a hint that they secretly commend the Conservatives for the big breakthrough in English decentralisation policy in the 1980s. One might wonder whether these impressive policies are achieved because or despite of law-based reform? Obviously, these headteachers are the product of two decades of decentralisation policy. They feel that Labour's close contact, regulation, and supervision are an improvement on Conservative free market policies that brought with them a sense of abandonment. But they are still sceptical about whether it is the reform alone, the law alone, that led them to these achievements. Perhaps this could not have been done without surplus funds and affluent neighbourhoods. The next chapter shows how principals with less fortunate surroundings cope with law-based reform.

4 Strong laws – weak schools: inner city schools' headteachers and their struggle for equity under the law

Four schools and one Education Action Zone (EAZ) are presented in this chapter. They are schools situated in poor surroundings, all in inner city areas – a distinct category of heads and schools in this study. Two are inner city primary schools which have a large immigrant and refugee intake. One is a large comprehensive secondary school in a poor area with a large black population. The fourth is a Catholic primary, voluntary aided school in an urban renewal area. The headteachers in these schools have great expectations from law-based reform in the late 1990s and early years of the twenty-first century. They see themselves as 'refugees' from the Conservative era, and expect a Labour government to strengthen them in face of wild competition and a fierce market situation. Basically, they are Labour supporters and voters. They see Labour as 'their' representatives, and 'their' government. They all speak quite freely about politics, which is a remarkable phenomenon. The stories of these headteachers show whether these expectations have been fulfilled, and how.

Case 1 High-rise – high hopes: how a majority–minority school copes with law-based reform

Gill's school is an eight-year primary, situated in a rundown neighbourhood in a big city. Some 250 students attend this school; 65 per cent of them receive 'free school meals' (equivalent to lunch tickets in the US) – an indication that they come from poor families. According to Gill, between them the children and their parents speak over twenty different languages (not including English). Most of the students come from immigrant and refugee families: some from various African countries, some from the Caribbean, some from former Yugoslavia, many of Bengali origin. They are Muslims, Hindus, Christians, and Buddhists. Some pupils 'appear' in the school in mid-year, whenever their parents arrive in England and in the neighbourhood. Other pupils disappear from the school suddenly – sometimes overnight, if they have to leave the area for fear of immigration officers. As part of the decentralisation process in England, formalised in the 1988 Education Reform Act, the school has nearly complete control over its entire budget – some £1,500,000 per annum (which includes teachers' and other staff salaries). The area had known better days. Recently, some urban renewal projects have emerged, though these include enclosed compounds of expensive ultra-modern townhouses that are bought by high-income young professionals who anticipate that property prices in the area will soar in the future. Right now, there are many closed shops with boarded entrances, homeless people asleep in their abandoned doorways. The entrance to the school, an old red-brick building, has a heavy metal door with CCTV. Beyond that, there is a rectangular corridor with a second door and further locked doors that lead into the administration area and into the class area itself. The building is in such bad shape that when one walks through the halls it seems that only age-old tradition, along with the caring hand of the staff, keep the walls together and the plaster hanging on. Gill, the head-teacher, is a young man, who has a master's degree in educational adminis-tration from a top-five university. Before becoming a headteacher, Gill was deputy head in another school, and a teacher for a few years. As I was impressed by the elaborate security system Gill said: 'We got some funding after a good OFSTED result to have a new and accessible safer office.'

Gill's office is open and comfortable. Instead of the traditional 'execu-tive'-type desk facing the newcomer, his desk faces the wall, as in a home study. In the corner, a sitting area includes three armchairs and a small coffee table. Gill's desk is scattered with technology: a desktop computer connected to a personal organiser on one side and a cellular phone on the other side. Gill has a lot to say about law-based reform, especially from the multicultural and multiracial aspects:

> In this system, we are very tight to the law with National Curriculum. It's impossible to work outside National Curriculum and it's frustrating because here you have to give basic life skills first. Numeracy and literacy are fine.

Gill highlights the problems of running a school where quite a few children speak only a little English. On the one hand, he feels committed to advancing the pupils towards national standards as expressed in the National Curriculum and PANDAs. On the other hand, he feels committed to the heritage, religion, and language that the pupils brought with them to England or experience at home or in their neighbourhood.

On my first visit to the school, I arrived in the middle of a typical maintenance crisis: occasionally, the drinking water becomes contaminated with sewage. The water system is rotten and should be replaced, but there is no money for this. Gill remarks, rather dryly, that perhaps the authorities think that most of the school's students are somewhat used to drinking sewage in their countries of origin, or else something would have been done about it by the authorities. Under the various laws and policies, the school should, theoretically, be able to replace the water system on its own budget. But this would cost some £150,000, which the school cannot afford. The government has come up with several solutions for such schools – some of which are quite amazing. For instance, the schools can retain the services of a finance and labour-supply company. When a school liaises with such a company, it signs over to the company its yearly budget for several years ahead. The company, in its turn, takes up a loan from a bank to replace the water system. In exchange, the company supplies the school with various services beginning with perhaps the obvious, such as cleaning and security, on to ICT equipment and maintenance, and finally even teachers and specialists. The school might practically lose the financial and organisational autonomy that was the original aim of primary legislation since the late 1980s. Although the school is not formally a part of an Education Action Zone, because the borough has not been selected as such, it does receive additional aid:

We just had funding for learners support centre and learning mentors. Our LEA has been identified as an area of need, a mini-EAZ, 6 primaries and then 2 LEAs put a bid for 15 primaries in deprived area so we have learning mentors. There's a big role for an LEA in co-ordinating the support for this area. I can't see it functioning without this. There's no consistency between LEAs as far as school finance goes. This isn't fair. There isn't a base that each school and school are entitled to. I was in conference and met other heads – some have half the money we have, and some double – and it's unfair. There is no equity in the system. Last year we had government money, a standards fund of £9,000 for school mentoring. They get DfEE money and council tax money.

So the law creates frameworks of free market coupled with centralised policy (Glatter 2002) of all sorts, ending in a situation where Gill's school is not autonomous but rather in a vice. He says:

I like to think that the standard of education is rising, and I'd like to think that children have higher aspirations that translate into self-motivation and improving, and that families know that they can succeed in what they want to do and in breaking the cycle of deprivation in these neighbourhoods, and it's not only education. It's housing and not this moving in and moving on. The law paints a picture but nobody is seeing the whole picture. The law sends a mixed message – on the one hand autonomy; on the other hand, a feeling of mistrust. I'd change the ministry's attitude towards schools – trusting schools and making the inspection process more supportive rather than punitive.

When discussing the hierarchy in the system, Gill finds that law-based reform's role in redefining the structure, and relations of units and levels within it, is problematic:

My boss is the governing body. They have legal responsibility to oversee my work. But I think our school also works very closely with the LEA. We've had good support. I had this issue with this governor and had to seek legal advice from the LEA. The LEAs are under pressure from the DfEE and the borough. They are a good LEA – that's what my thesis is about – and I know that the LEA is very important.

The introduction of a governing body is a big change in Gill's concept of accountability. From an LEA school that had very little control over its resources, it went to a school with much more independence:

> Governing bodies are a good idea but there is so much paperwork. It's like another job. There are seven committees that meet twice a term. I think the governing body has too much to do, so it is a safeguard. When I was a deputy I sat on committees but now I'm advertising so it's difficult.

Which brings Gill to broaden his scope and talk of the system as a whole:

> I think the change that has happened in the last ten years or so is for the better. Accountability is right. They don't have the right balance yet. League tables are a waste of time. Heads and teachers being account- able and governors being accountable is good because in many schools pupils were receiving bad education. We were at the bottom of the league table 3, not because we were a bad school but because it's a bad area and children were coming in year 6 and were not able to do national tests. OFSTED could be better: the amount of paperwork, time and stress put into the inspection is huge. We got a good OFSTED, and we balanced it, but there should be another way. If there is a good LEA they know which school is good and their inspection findings can be used and schools can do their own inspection, and they should look at all of those, and if there are any grey areas they should look at these in more detail. They should incorporate all of this and talk to the head- teacher and make it less intimidating. We evaluate all the time, we do our own observations, and more schools do that over time.

Gill thinks the system should not just audit and expect things to change because of this, but should offer actual tools and structures for schools like his own. For instance, the need to strengthen such schools should be recognised and it should be understood that what such schools need is not just more money (which is scarce, anyway) but different support mecha- nisms, different standards, and different relations between the sub-units in the system. For instance, the models of school autonomy cannot, according to Gill, be uniform for all types of schools. Also, the governing body in well-to-do areas can provide completely different types of support than the governing body in a school and neighbourhood like Gill's. One possible structure that is relevant for such a school is known as a 'one stop shop':

> There's this social policy, this action zone. Putting education with social services and housing, there are masses of money going in and it's not cohesive. I was in a school in Harlem [NYC] and they have their own social worker and school club. I'd change the DfEE attitude towards schools – trusting schools, and the inspection process should be more supportive rather than punitive. I do politics and pedagogy. My fundamental claim is that the pupils get what they deserve but I do both really. I'm very active in the LEA and in the school with the parents. You've got to be an executive officer, but you should know why you are doing this, and what children need for you to base your philosophies on – I took a course in London city airport and I knew what these people know and more although I manage only a million and a half budget and only 50+ staff.

The main criticism that Gill has towards law-based reform in England's school system is that is divides between types of schools – strengthening the strong and weakening the weak. The law is a type of scaffold for reform – it helps in implementation and preservation of change. Policy makers sometimes tend to think headteachers are conservative and afraid of change, and will not co-operate without a legal mandate.

Case 2 Inner city – outer limits: a tough school in a tougher neighbourhood

Ken, another principal in an urban renewal area, who runs a large, split-site 1,200 pupil secondary school, sees the law simply as a divider between schools:

> On the one hand, the law makes education the absolute theme of central government. It's an important statement. But sometimes I feel that some has not been planned, just sending endless lists of initiatives that have

not been thought about. There is a serious issue of teacher recruitment that central government is ignoring.... In the sense that there has been a shift of responsibility to heads and their performance and part of me is with that, but I want a government that is sympathetic and doesn't just expect improvement year by year. I mean I was shouting like crazy on bureaucracy but getting it to the hoof – government is not enough into structures. They hint what they want but don't go all the way. They talk on integration but keep grammar schools because there is more money in them.

Ken's is a typical inner city secondary school that can be found in big cities in many western countries. It is a black-dominated area. In a way, it is perhaps even tougher than immigrant areas because the neighbourhood is characterised by second or third generation deprivation, exclusion, dispossession, and marginalisation. Ken thinks inner city schools are not treated fairly by the current law-based reform. He feels the law burdens schools like his own with new requirements, and creates market-like frameworks that force his school to compete in a game using an unfair set of rules. The government itself competes with Ken's school either by opening snazzy 16–19 colleges that receive all the facilities Ken's school cannot afford, or by retaining posh government-owned and run grammar schools:

> I think over the time the whole process of LMS and inspections and league tables have destroyed inner city schools and drained talent so it's not more equitable and the government is trying to redress what it has done wrong. The government recognises what is a trend outside education so it is actually trying to do something, but I'm doubtful whether it really can.

Ken explains that he put in three years of huge efforts to recruit quality teachers from well-to-do areas in the city to work in his school. Some of these teachers are young graduates with Masters degrees in natural sciences, in mathematics, in history, and in English, from top universities. They were 'lured' to Ken's school with promises of fast-track promotion to heads of departments and preparing the sixthformers for GCSEs and

A levels. But now that the sixth-form college is around the corner, these new talented academics are becoming restless. On top of this, Ken is worried by the fact that he sees the school disintegrating when the older, better pupils who act as role models for younger students and often siblings, might move out from his school. He explains:

> I feel clearly under pressure from the teachers. The greatest pressure is about accountability to results and maintaining level 5 on SATs and GCSEs. This is the greatest pressure. Funny enough I can't see anyone particularly who is the boss. In terms of numbers who want to come to the school, numbers into the sixth form I mean, my concern is if I can maintain these indicators of improvement. But if I don't do that, I would feel pressure from the LEA because I wouldn't be contributing to their target. The interesting thing is that at the moment it is the sixth form, because they want to set up a 16 to 19 institution. The government will push us – whether they can steamroll us or whether the coalition of parents and pupils will fight this out. One thing is, it's not across the borough and a school with a sixth form is considered better and if you want to retain teachers. We would have a terrible period of transition. What will happen to those who teach sixth form? You have a better chance to recruit a physicist if he can teach A levels. On my senior management team we have two deputies in charge of both buildings and four senior teachers and one who runs the sixth-form consortium, and each one has a variety of other roles such as co-ordinating heads of year, performance management, funding, bidding for grants, we made a lot of money out of that. The senior teachers are into citizenship, it's a new government initiative, on top of gifted and talented programmes, teaching and learning strategies, and exams, and another for basic skills, and one for cover staff arrangements and ICT network. The senior teachers were chosen by external advert and others were promoted by me and the governors.

Ken's situation is extremely complicated, not to say somewhat chaotic:

> I've been a head through the changes: heads being in charge of curriculum and pupil behaviour to a manager who's in charge of the general running in the school to have that sense of control. I would have

welcomed more training and when the National Curriculum came, for formal training. I would have dealt with this more adequately, but becoming locally managed it seemed to be possible to effect change, but this may be easier than before. Simple things like painting the school, you wouldn't have to wait seven years for the cycle. Issues like staffing and finance, adding another class, to make classes smaller, assistance staff, and forming the identity of your school, extra librarians, or how to concentrate your administrative staff. In terms of the senior management team, we are a split-site school and as we got bigger, we could ensure that we had proper representation in both buildings. It had freed us from constraints. I had more opportunities to determine who gets paid more.

Ken emphasises that his role has changed substantially because of law-based reform. This is perhaps an argument against what has been written in Chapter 2, regarding the lack of legislation that deals specifically with headteachers. It is a fact, and not only in Ken's story but in that of many other headteachers, that their role has indeed changed dramatically, without legislation. But it is exactly a story like Ken's that emphasises why such legislation is required. Everyone received formal power except the headteacher. This leaves him or her running around, grasping at authority, which should have been delegated formally.

As the LEA became more distant and there was a possibility to break away and become a GM school and we didn't. In fact, no one did because the LEA addressed the needs of the school and had a specific funding for children with special needs. The changes that happened to us – we were a school deep in a regeneration area, 'city challenge', and we could use this for additional funding and the fabric of the building which made it attractive to parents, and we doubled our intake. It's been a difficult time because on the one hand, you were your own boss, but on the other hand, you were pinned down by the National Curriculum that was cumbersome and bureaucratic, and by OFSTED so there was more government control, that pinned us down. Being an inner city school we are very much fearful of things like league tables so while we went out from the LEA the pressure of accountability became much more severe as central government took a much greater role in education.

Again, like others, Ken is bewildered by the mass of government initiatives:

> They hint what they want but don't go all the way. They talk on integration but keep grammar schools. There is more money, but it's targeted to government initiatives such as gifted pupils, while others are left behind. Of course I do my best to take advantage of these initiatives: we've been given £65,000 for learning mentors and £100,000 for our new behavioural centres. They don't allow you to improve according to *your* agenda, but according to government agenda. Literacy and numeracy are moving now to secondary schools. I agree you have to raise standards, but it hurts teacher autonomy and what heads are. Both ends of the spectrum, neither is right. Once teachers were ill-prepared, but now we do have targets and schemes of work, but teachers become automated and it's maintaining that balance between proper inspection and autonomy. The schools are certainly very different now and you feel much more pressurised. And if you feel more pressurised without financial or professional reward, this causes burnout in management and teachers.

As in other schools, Ken sees his immediate alliance in the school's governing body:

> The board of governors always had very positive relations with me and with school management. Both chairs have been very supportive. Perhaps in a sense they are leaving a lot to us. In my case, they have been supportive, and have helped a lot. The governing body acts as a sort of critical friend.

Ken points to the correlation between law-based reform and school leadership, or perhaps the close connection between a whole system change and what actually goes on inside schools:

> I think over the time the whole process of LMS, inspections, and league tables have destroyed inner city schools and drained talent, so it's not more equitable, but less. The government is trying to redress what it's done wrong, there is a conference on schools which have over 50 per cent free school meals. The government recognises what is a trend

outside education, so it is actually trying to do something, but I'm doubtful whether it really can. My job has genuinely become much more complex and it has to be redefined because it seems undoable. Heads are putting in more hours. We have an administrator who is a senior secretary and we need a higher staff member. We don't know if the head is manager or a teaching headteacher. Sometimes I think we haven't been radical enough.

Case 3 Halfway from home: Khanum Mia's battle for better schooling

On a socio-economic scale, Khanum Mia's school is situated somewhere close to Gill's. It is an old former middle-class-presently-underclass neighbourhood. The area looks a bit more respectable than Gill's: small two-storey townhouses, some gardens, and some shops – open and functioning. Khanum Mia, the head, is a Hindu woman in her early forties. She is very experienced having already worked in five different schools. Previously she was a teacher, then cluster leader, went on to deputy head in one school and headteacher in another – this one being her second headship, already going on for the fifth year:

> I'll start with by saying that over the years I have no doubt in my mind that I'm the educational leader of this establishment so educational law effects me but doesn't control me. If you'd inspect my school, we are accountable about everything. I've always been accountable but the question is to whom. I love a governing body that is critical but before the governing body, I carry my staff and my parents so although I like my governing body the professional group is more important – I do it to cover my back, as I'm an employee of the school. It's the same with the general inspector of the school. Let's look at literacy strategy and numeracy strategy. For two years, I've lived with it to the letter but two years down the line I've asked for an inspection of what's going on in the school so we'll have a good thrashing. So it's about me knowing. And if I don't think it's good, we'll change it. We'll get support and advice from other professionals and then adapt to suit our children.

This trend of 'covering one's back' and actually playing between the various powers in and around the school is common to most heads interviewed in this study. The heads 'map' the arena, identify relevant figures or bodies and plan a strategy for having as many as possible on their side. For instance, although according to law, the governing body is responsible, Khanum Mia established and is managing a separate relationship with pupils' parents. This is not only to balance the power of the governing body but also out of concern that the governing body does not always offer comprehensive representation for the parents. The parents are seen as a type of 'constituency' and also the ones responsible directly for each and every child's education and therefore she sees herself as accountable to them and not only to the governing body.

Khanum Mia is an obsessive consumer of knowledge, taking part both in the LPSH programme, and numerous courses, and lately has taken up a Masters degree in a very good nearby university. She is well informed on all innovations in the field of educational leadership and administration. The school is struggling in a problematic area, and competing with a local voluntary aided school of faith that has more funds and can afford to be much more selective about its student body. Khanum Mia's school has an LEA-assigned and mandatory intake – that is, a catchment area. Another area that Khanum Mia sees as immanent to her job is the area of school finance. She sees school law as a tool that defines and frames the financial opportunities and sources that are available to the headteacher and the school:

> I came in at the point of autonomy. I always had total autonomy about the budget. I like my job and I always had total autonomy, if you look at my predecessor he was a *** but he accumulated lots of funds that he hadn't used. So I had surplus funds I could use, and did use, because I thought I should improve things with money. This school is an LEA school, but it's different than it used to be because schools like this one now have much more autonomy than they used to. But we still get a lot of services from the council – dependent or supportive – take your pick.

Khanum Mia explains that the financial planning of things is an important function of the head. Educational law assists her in the enforcement of working standards:

> I found out that they were actually teaching five hours less than they were supposed to! Can you imagine that? But they accepted it because it's the law. Teachers were planning but no one looked at it. We built a plan with the staff. We had 28 objectives and you know when they teach education they say this is too much but we got all of them because the main title was what does this do to learning.

This example is proof of the success of local management of schools, a major characteristic of law-based reform in England since the mid-1980s (Levacic 1995). Statutory budgetary self-control and autonomy coupled with free market as a regulatory mechanism, prompts heads like Khanum Mia to open a debate on age-old arrangements within the school. Such arrangements are often contradictory to school targets and policy but are the result of 'estates', 'franchises', and 'vested rights and interests' of power groups within the school. This is an example of how law-based reform creates a brand new arena for heads to operate within. Under this framework heads reorganise their schools, and their resources. They 'rattle the cage' in an attempt to improve and strengthen the connection, or perhaps correlation, between what the school wishes to achieve, and the structure, resource allocation, human resource management, and so on:

> The other thing is the budget. We have foreign language courses in the evenings. It's not hidden, but it's part of the school curriculum. The first year I got money from a local college. The second year we needed £5,000 and I begged – I went from shop to shop and got nothing so I brought it to the governors, knowing they would say you can't have that. But I brought them proof – not statistical – because it ran only one year but I presented case studies and today this is part of school budget.

In these words, Khanum Mia exemplifies how schools in England actually define the boundaries of their work, including active participation in locating new types and new sources for expanding their budget along with choosing new areas of operation for the school. Thus, Khanum Mia expands the market in which her school operates, provides further opportunities for the school, offers a new horizon for the school, and strengthens the school's chance for survival in case of an unexpected drop in enrolment, sudden budget changes, and other unexpected hazards. At the same time, entering these new fields strengthens the traditional occupations of the school. For instance, in Khanum Mia's school, these new areas allow her to offer support for underachievers, offer a variety of programmes that supply the needs of the various ethnic or religious groups in the school, and offer clubs that cover all types of specific interests the children have. In times of budget tightening this is important for schools, especially when the parents cannot serve as an additional source of income:

> I do have classroom assistants who are parents or people from around here. It took me five years to teach my teachers not to use them for cleaning paint pots. We get additional funding for this and use some of the special needs budget and they work under the direction of the teacher and the special needs co-ordinator. Once upon a time, they wanted to stay with the same teacher or class. Over the years, I've simplified it for myself.

This does not mean that Khanum Mia is satisfied with how law-based reform creates reasonable working conditions for schools like her own:

> I think the funding system towards independent schools is quite unfair. My siblings have children in independent schools so I see the difference. There they see computers when they are four and here there is one for each classroom. An effective LEA makes my job easier with things like SAT results. All this is done by the LEA. But the leaders of tomorrow won't come from my school. They will come from all of these nice private schools around here.

This understanding represents the disappointment of headteachers in law-based reform. They really expected it to change England's socio-economic scene. Perhaps now they are realistic – or perhaps impatient. But all heads like Khanum Mia report of great enthusiasm for the reforms in the late 1990s, followed by a more realistic awareness of their limitations.

School auditing plays an important part in the professional life of a headteacher like Khanum Mia. Her ranking in these audits is crucial for the school's survival and ongoing development, as well as for her own personal tenure as headteacher of the school:

> I don't think the government would say OFSTED is a way of checking, but it's a question of how effective the team is. I always say I won't let them do things to us – but do things with us. We've had a bad experience last year. The inspection team had no understanding of inner city schools with a large minority population. They wrote down: 'there isn't any graffiti or vandalism' and then they found a health and safety risk on a set of steps where no child ever goes, but still they wouldn't listen. They never asked me what background I came from, but they asked some of my staff 'you have a head with an interesting name does she belong to one of your community groups?' The race issue is a big thing because there is a person here and a professional here. Before half term, my only Bangladeshi member of staff did something quite unprofessional and a member of my staff who's in charge of ethnic minority education said, 'I can't see that a member of our staff has resigned because of racism'. There was this poster that said 'we are here because you are there'. I've minimised the impact of it on one level because I can look anyone in the eye and say we at X school do our best to give a good education.

Khanum Mia's school takes advantage of new tools that school reform in England allows, including Excellence in Cities and Education Action Zones (EAZs).

> We've just worked to get EAZ money and had a consultant write a bid. It's been a nightmare but there are six schools altogether in this. And she couldn't grasp the idea of hard-to-reach families. So what we've done is create a mini-EAZ and the government provides us with some money together with the LEA.

Khanum Mia ends her story with a statement I've heard in several versions, from several heads that took part in this study: 'I really think the government has become a provider of information on education and not a provider of education any more.' This strong sentence is a declaration of abandonment. Despite the numerous tools that law-based reform offers to schools such as this – inner city schools in tough areas – there is still strong resentment among their heads.

Case 4 Amazing grace in Michael's school

Michael's is a small voluntary aided school in the neighbourhood next to Gill's. It strikingly highlights the contradictions and conflicts of urban renewal: does it renew the buildings or the population? Does it actually benefit the 'native' population of the area or does it overlook them when bulldozers and agile contractors swarm in? Michael's school is situated on a quiet street. On one side of the building, just in front of the entrance to the school, there is a brand new complex that advertises ultra-modern apartments for city Yuppies. On the other side, adjacent to the backyard of the school, are some abandoned buildings practically in ruins and inhabited by drug addicts and their suppliers. Michael recalls an absurd event when an anti-terrorist police unit launched a raid on these drug-related gangs from within his school's backyard – only to find out that the small, ragged, one-storey building is actually a school. This weird state of things is immanent to life in this school.

Michael depicts the hierarchy in which he operates: 'Well, I'm the headteacher. Right above me is the school governing body; above that is the archdiocese; above that is the Pope. Need I go on?' These words are somewhat surprising considering the poor conditions of the school, and they underline the power, sustainability, and self-confidence of head-teachers in voluntary aided (VA) and voluntary controlled (VC) schools. In a situation that is defined by a large number of the heads in this study as one of professional and personal loneliness, the heads of these schools stand out as beacons of self-assurance. Their relation to an organisation that is separate from the usual hierarchy of an LEA and government ministry (known currently as DfES) gives them additional power and of course additional funds. This affiliation offers a different contextual viewpoint than is available for the 'common' headteacher. Often it offers an additional professional community beyond the existing forums in LEAs, leadership centres, and such. When everything else is ambiguous, temporal and political, being part of such a group is literally a safe haven. Notwithstanding, the additional funds that are part of being such a school are quite important as well. Michael elaborates on the hierarchy:

> The governing body is the employer. They are a very high profile governing body. One of the things that changed enormously is the role of the governing body. Now I write a ten-page report all night. They are very professional; they are a real mix of high-powered professionals who have kids in the school. I wanted to make sure they are not just white New Labour yuppie types so I've recruited a black governor because we had 60 per cent black children. There are too many parents on it for it to be completely balanced, but right now it's OK. With staff and Church, it wasn't always like that, I had to get rid of a lot of people.

Michael indicates the areas where law-based reform is part of his work as headteacher in a school of faith:

> This is a very oversubscribed school. People have an artificial right of appeal. On the one hand we must keep class size below 30, but people appeal and give a sob story and then we end up with 32 to 33 in a class, which makes the law look ridiculous and you have high street lawyers looking for work. Then we have special needs and people are using litigation to pursue their rights. You can literally cross the road and see such differences [Michael is referring to the new high-rise project just across the street]. We review our admissions policy every year.

This is an important part of life in 'a school of faith'. Though often situated in tough neighbourhoods, in a way they are elitist institutions, at least within and in comparison with their immediate surroundings. Religious practice becomes a buffer used to control the school's intake:

> One parent or partner must be a practising Catholic and present a form signed by the priest and then we have a catchment area. Most of the area is very poor. All sorts of areas have special needs but the main problems are getting children to the eight stages of the special needs programme.

Perhaps the most important issue Michael mentions concerning recent law-based reform is staff management, recruitment, and control. Threshold assessment and performance management have changed his work, but there are still remains of the previous system in which the head had much less control over the main assets and tools for carrying out his or her responsibilities. Michael explains:

> Employment law affects us. We are moving into a much more Americanised society. People are taking grievances to the unions that are encouraging everyone to say they are stressed out. I was a union man myself. I play tennis but a lot of people manage their stress by lawsuits. This is a jackpot of racial and sex discrimination. I'm not talking only about teachers, but also about kitchen staff. Work practice has changed enormously in the last five years and I'm running out of legal aid. In one school I did serious stuff and have been under threats.

As tough and unrelenting as he is on the issue of being able to build a quality staff, Michael is much more lenient when it comes to using performance management as a tool of control. Once he has good teachers, he feels he should treat them in a fair way:

> I try to get a good atmosphere so teachers come here. They just hear about the school. I don't put pressure on teachers. I don't ask for plans. It's such a boring life for teachers making all their plans. So as long as people do their work I'm not into monitoring them. A lot of heads are going mad and bullying their staff because of initiative overload. I had a teacher who applied for threshold assessment. It took me about half an hour doing each one. I wrote: 'I agree with what they wrote, she's a good teacher.' I'm not giving myself a hard time. I was in the training and people there were all into looking at the course they had in 1973. You know Goldman's theory is about tough companies who learned that treating staff with dignity is good for the bottom line and we're not in a bottom line business, we're into spiritual and intellectual well-being. I met someone who told me 'I knew your head, she's very nice' and then she said, 'no she's a bully'. So a lot of heads have these devious ways of controlling the teachers and we will need lawyers because of sex discrimination lawsuits but this is a nods and winks thing. A way to

give more nineties [per cent as part of teachers' performance management scheme] to more staff and justify it.

This is an example of the non-linear quality of educational policy (Ball
1994) that probably amazes policy makers repeatedly. No matter how
strict and elaborate the law is, what actually happens when a headteacher's
ideology has an influence is a different story. Michael believes that his
entire teacher workforce should receive the additional money, and that
making detailed teaching plans is an unnecessary chore. Perhaps the fact
that he is not a government employee gives him additional power.

Like many other headteachers who took part in this study, politics are
part of Michael's point of view on education and law-based reform:

> The government gives all kinds of initiatives. Blair did send his kids to
> a local Catholic primary. He is passionately interested in education. The
> government comes in [was elected] for all sorts of reasons but they
> genuinely meant it when they say education. A lot of the ministers have
> young children and then they saw Singapore and thought all of us will
> be high-tech workers. They saw a massive skills gap especially in
> Holland and Germany. They set targets that filtered down to the local
> authority that implements it in schools. The government says 'inter-
> vention proportionate to success' so we didn't get a lot of that before.

By saying this, Michael refers to the 1997 *Excellence in Schools* government White Paper on educational policy. He is content with his
autonomous role as head and with the need to compete, but still has fears
due to lack of resources:

> They leave you alone. There's a lot more money. Money is good. It's been
> a huge improvement, the big problem being no teachers. Monday morn-
> ing you have this churning in your stomach – who will arrive?
> Especially supply teachers. There's a school down the road with eight sup-
> ply teachers and all of them have to be trained in numeracy and literacy.

Michael talks about his role as leader in his school:

> It's evolved over the years. OFSTED says you should develop your
> middle management. But in such a small school, there is a head and a

deputy and all the rest are middle management. I believe in this trian-
gulation of parents, Church, and school. People get together one day a
week and I try to run the school in the same way. I'm in lead, I'm in
charge, but I ask everyone to take part. I have a terrific early years
manager and my Key Stage manager needed a lot of training. She is a
tough foreign lady who learned a lot. Being a man in a predominantly
female environment and telling a woman to do something, being a single
parent, I must be sensitive. Once I asked people to get to the point but
I've learned be a much better listener.

Undoubtedly, headteachers like Gill, Ken, Khanum Mia, and Michael
are educational leaders who move with (not against) the times. They understand what is going on, but do not necessarily accept it quietly. They see
themselves as social advocates, understand that education is a political
issue, and do not hesitate to utilise politics to advance the interests of
their schools, along with their own careers as educational leaders. This is
also why Michael sees his responsibilities as stretched out beyond the
boundaries of the school, although not without the odd reservation: 'I did
a lot for the borough but then I said "hang in – who am I working for?"
So I did the odd mentoring or inspection. But most of my work is here.'

Once again, the story of Michael's school is representative of English
schools and their leaders, especially in inner cities. First, they see Labour
government as 'their' government, hence they are sympathetic towards
its policies, but also have great expectations. Torn between new managerial ideas on leadership and educational administration, and egalitarian
ideas on social justice and fair distribution of social goods, the headteachers voice their concern and criticism about law-based reform since
1997. They highlight the differences between policy under the Conservatives and under Labour, and then again think that not enough is done for
inner city schools. One thing is clear: they are not passive – they are
strong leaders who redefine leadership through an exploration and understanding of educational policy and law-based reform in England:

> This society is changing and it is so good. Hague [former leader of the
> Conservative party] lived in north Yorkshire where you don't have non-
> whites unless they run the cleaners. In the 1980s, it was some kind of

apartheid. I genuinely think education has improved in the last five years. I did my training in the 1970s when you had like a carousel of ten different activities going on at the same time. Teachers could teach whatever they wanted. There were no standards. We let down a generation of black people in the 1970s and 1980s – kids who needed to sit down and work were allowed to express themselves, and in the urban area, kids need structure. I think we needed much more structured teaching of maths and English. The league tables are terrible. The National Curriculum was very important. But overall, the system has changed for the better.

Educational action: is there hope for the 'socialist few' within the zone?

This final part of the chapter presents impressions and interpretations from a visit to two Education Action Zones, in big city neighbourhoods that are known to be some of the most problematic in England. In this one story, the headquarters of an EAZ will be presented vis-à-vis one of the schools – as briefly as possible. Views of EAZ officials are presented as well. There is a striking contrast between the headquarters of the project and the reality in one of its schools.

The headquarters of the EAZ is a smart modern building, which is in striking contrast to the rundown area in which the headquarters are located. An enclosed car park for the EAZ's workers welcomes the visitor into a reception area on the ground floor. This floor is divided into two parts. The first part includes a bank-type counter. In front of this counter a weaving line of citizens – prospective students' parents – are waiting for service. Interpreters stand beside the secretaries and a quick check reveals that only a few of the conversations are in English. At the outskirts of this reception area, a few empty offices await EAZ officials, who use them to meet their clients. In the middle of this large hall, an electronic barrier manned by a security guard prevents the citizens of the zone from entering the building itself. Once this barrier is crossed, the visitor leaves the hustle and bustle of the reception area and enters an enclave of tranquillity, efficiency, and professionalism. Here you will find numerous offices, brand new, with state-of-the-art computer equipment, and smart furniture. The citizens, the direct clients of the zone, cannot enter the building, and the EAZ officials come down to meet with them in the offices in the reception area. This system is not unique to the zone, and can be found in other government or local human services headquarters. Nevertheless, it still makes a statement, even if not intentionally, with the parents crowded in the lobby and the quiet on the upper floors.

Christine, the headteacher of a primary school in the same EAZ, sees it as a mixed blessing. Her school is on one side of a street with small two-storey Victorian black-brick buildings. A high-wired fence surrounds the school. The gate that opens into the schoolyard is a heavy-set metal door with CCTV, and then again the same surveillance system can be found at the main building. The building is very old and the halls are badly in need of renovation. Some new ICT equipment is scattered in classes. Christine says:

> The government doesn't think of itself as the sole provider of education. It's responsible for standards and monitoring those who do it. We heads are the socialist few. Look at this EAZ: I get a lot of money from them, but we were forced to get together and produce such detailed programmes and employ an expert out of our own budget. The EAZ has this new building – the only decent one in the borough. We're about to go to a private finance initiative. I get furious letters from unions. But it's the only way to get money to the school. They'll run it, clean it, develop it, and secure it. In the first five years, they invest money in the building and it's a 25-year contract. The profit will come in the eighteenth year. Will the EAZ still be around? Pragmatically, I can't get the gutters fixed. I have a fast Internet line. First, it's already far from enough. Second, will I be able to pay for it once the EAZ is gone? I doubt it!

Christine outlines her fears and hopes for EAZs. One of the problems is that headteachers in areas like Christine's are weary of initiatives and promises. Each time a new idea comes up, they muster the resources, boost staff morale, and hope for the best, only to be disappointed. This observation is not only a criticism of law-based reform under Labour; it is a worldwide finding from numerous studies on educational reform (MacDonald 1991):

> Local management of schools and the National Curriculum were the big change. We just got a big grant from Excellence in Cities to begin a learning support centre. How does this coincide or collide with the EAZ? I like the autonomy. The school is better run since LMS. I like doing the budget – though it's a lot of work. But I think there is place for the LEA. I wouldn't go the Tory way of abolishing LEAs altogether. From my view, collaboration and co-operation are important, we shouldn't be fighting each other. The LEA isn't always efficient, but it represents the people. How does the EAZ fit into this? For example, we went to an independent staff provider. They cost half and are just as inefficient. LEAs have a role in supporting schools. They tried to set up a school development advisory model but it didn't work. Advisors are making good money. Groups of schools that have common characteristics. I lead the school in a different way. My job has changed. It's obviously different being in charge of the budget, having control of the building – but now the EAZ brings in money. Will it ask for control?

The vulnerability of the inner city school headteacher in a poor area is presented here at its worst: need for change – fear of change; self-efficacy – powerlessness; a sense of hope – a sense of despair. EAZs are responsible for this when they enter the area. This background may serve as a mitigating factor when judging EAZs as part of law-based reform, but it also means that they have to be extremely sensitive. Condescending 'we know it all and are going to set things straight' attitudes are not helpful at all.

When interviewing EAZ officials the picture became even more complicated:

> The idea of EAZs is to raise achievement and reduce deprivation in bad areas. Some money is set aside for EAZs. However, hardly any EAZ has acted outside its statutory area, because these are the most problematic around employment of teachers and governing bodies. An EAZ can change national employment requirement and the government thought this is more exciting. I think they are actually trying to break the unions,

have them work more hours for more money. But hardly any EAZ did that because their teachers were working flat out already so this was hardly done. Our schools joined the EAZ knowing that working standards wouldn't change. They thought teachers will work longer days and have less vacations. They are stressed out to the eyeballs. Most staff are prepared to run an activity after hours once a week, but they won't do that every day because they would burn out. As for governing bodies, they were supposed to surrender their powers to the EAZ but no one did this in the country. No governing bodies would do this if they had any sense of pride.... The main way we promote higher achievement and less social exclusion is through programmes and we have additional funding. When I was a head for 11 years....What I thought the idea is to create an emerging dynamic within school. I saw the school as a mini-EAZ. I wanted to work with my neighbouring schools in the primary sector in particular, and with businesses and my community and generate income. Every head should do that. This was good practice promotion. So EAZs help you do something you should have or could have done in any case. Combined with other initiatives there might be an outcome when there is an initiative to maintain the exclusivity of middle class. People like Chris Woodhead [former HM Chief Inspector of Schools and head of OFSTED] were talking like this. When the level went up, they made it harder. People talk of a gold standard, which is protecting elitist groups.

This means EAZs are about power and politics, and not only about promoting education. But they are also an impressive tool to create new sources of money, and perhaps, as the following statement shows, introduce some new managerial practices into schools in decaying areas:

Education is a complex and complicated issue and the only chance that young people in poverty can better themselves, so having democratic involvement is important, but business gives new ideas like private leadership partnerships where heads link with corporate managers and learn on finance and business and business people, and have learned on multi-skilled approach and the complexity and intricacy of their job. One of the things a headteacher said here is that having a business partner was a good thing because it gave her the courage to bend the rules.

I think the government has carefully ensured that business is just complementary. Anyone who accuses Michael Barber [former senior Teachers' Union official, currently Head of Standards and Effectiveness Unit, DfEE] of not caring for the provision of education is wrong. The initiatives are coming from the government! They have the aim of raising achievement and increasing social inclusion. This is a global dichotomy – some people have more money and others are in poverty. We might have a two-tier education, private education for the rich. EAZs balance this a bit by equal funding in inner cities, where there is a massive set of impossible economic and social conditions. We cannot afford having schools with 5 per cent GCSEs and it's not because teachers are not working hard, it's because there is some ideological teacher who should have been updated and is unaware of recent developments that can change achievement levels. It's an issue of recruitment and here they had the lowest performance management. We should give teachers more support: housing and travel cards. We should engage parents who are apathetic and antagonistic towards education. It was Bernstein who said, 'you cannot compensate for society'. We should be careful how much of a social engineer we should be.

This passionate monologue is typical of the ambivalence EAZs cause. They offer a mixture of high hopes and fears; a cleaner approach to education as opposed to the most common political power struggles, not to mention the bad experience with faddism that wears off and leaves the underprivileged in the same shape, or worse.

Several questions arise on EAZs:

1. How do EAZs coincide with LEAs? How are co-operation and control issues over schools organised between the two authorities?
2. How are EAZs empowering schools? How are they incorporated into the overall law-based reform of LMS? What happens with contradictions between the two?
3. What is the lifespan of EAZs, and how will schools in low-income areas be able to cope with the upgrade of their conditions after the EAZ expires?

4. How are the private economic aspects of EAZs planned and controlled, concerning school financial autonomy?
5. Finally, how can EAZs be presented as more user-friendly and democratic, and less condescending?

This study is not an analysis of the policy issues of EAZs and similar initiatives, but shows how the headteachers view EAZs.

5 English law-based reform in the eyes of headteachers: an overall view of empirical findings and theoretical concepts

Plan of the chapter: headteachers' views on law-based reform

Chapters 3 and 4 presented complete headteacher and school stories on law-based reform. This was a first-level analysis. The current chapter attempts to paint a picture for the reader on how law-based reform in England under the Labour government is seen through the eyes of all the headteachers that took part in this study. The sample, as detailed in the Appendix, includes headteachers who were visited in their schools, as well as other headteachers who completed an open questionnaire on law-based reform. The analysis, on which this chapter is based, is a second-degree analysis. Codification and categorisation of headteachers' statements are the material used here. The complete data were 'cut up' according to the categories. The first parts show how headteachers look at England's school system, its structure, and its components. It then goes on to show how headteachers differentiate among different types of educational law. Finally, the chapter shows how different 'types' of headteachers (classified according to SES of their schools, inner city or suburban, secondary or primary, etc.) address law-based reform.

Mapping law-based reform by headteachers

Data analysis produced a list of law-related issues that headteachers address in their work. The issues are, in descending order of significance:[1]

1. The National Curriculum.
2. Performance Management, teachers' pay, recruitment, and redundancy.
3. Admissions, catchment areas, enrolment policy, and appeal mechanisms.

4. Governing bodies.
5. Exclusions and retention.
6. Standards, school inspections, OFSTED, SATs, PANDAs, Key Stages.
7. General workload for headteachers, government bureaucracy and its influence on headteachers' roles.
8. Parents' rights and parents' involvement in schools.
9. Budget management and legal aid.

Three further issues also came up:

1. Special educational needs (SEN) – statements, funding, etc.
2. Health and safety in schools.
3. Bullying, violence, and behaviour/anger management.

These issues are not examined per se in this volume but are mentioned in connection with other issues, such as 'budget neutral' policy and school autonomy.

The politics of law-based reform

Figure 5.1 shows the headteachers' mindscapes on educational law in England. The main finding here regards the connection between educational law and politics, as perceived by headteachers.

First, the mindscape shows, according to the headteachers, that nearly every aspect of schooling in England is law-based and regulated. The headteachers differentiate between legal issues that they define as 'totally' legal, and legal issues that they see as 'political'. Among the political are issues such as enrolment policy (including catchment areas), admissions, and appeals; permanent exclusions, legislation on school finance (e.g. funding formulas); and OFSTED and other standardised tools like PANDAs, SATs, and Key Stages. All of these come under the heading of 'free market' school choice, which also includes the introduction of sixth-form colleges, specialist, CTC, and beacon schools. All headteachers in this study welcome open enrolment policy and are more than willing to

Figure 5.1 *How principals in England view educational law and its relation to politics*

Head's Legal and political 'mindscapes'

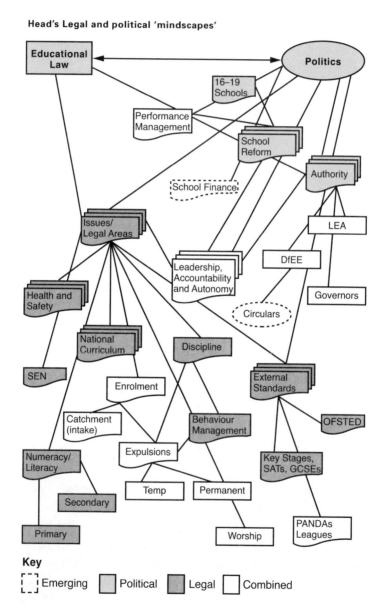

Key

`[- - -]` Emerging   ▢ Political   ▢ Legal   ▢ Combined

take part in open competition. Their major worry, however, is that the game should be a fair one; and according to the headteachers it is government's responsibility to ensure this. This view sees government as a regulator. For instance, the headteachers see government legislation that cracks down on permanent exclusions and on dropout rates (especially in secondary schools) as political, while legislation that deals with 'behaviour management' is perceived as a 'purely legal' policy, targeted at helping students who are on the verge of being expelled. The headteachers think that a mechanism designed for lessening disruptive behaviour and which actually assists them in reducing exclusions, is straightforward and sincere. Of course, the fact that this policy is accompanied by funds, ideas, programmes, and so on, is part of what steers their opinion. The same can be said of OFSTED and audit systems in general. The headteachers are not inherently against it; they just have some reservations:

> All central measurements of school success based on SATs, data for PANDAs, etc., KS2, place staff under immense pressures to teach to the tests. Summative assessment of this type does not equate high standards of teaching and learning. The key purpose of my job is to create optimum learning environment. The tests lessen my ability to do this. Target setting has sharpened the focus on raising standards. Publication could be difficult if targets aren't met, but I do feel this has a positive influence overall. But again, trainings have been slow and rather delayed. However, I do feel we're further advanced with this.

> The inspection process is demoralising for staff. It leads to unnecessary stress and pressure. It knocks those already down and causes upset in the wider professional community. I do not feel this helps towards achieving schools' aims – I feel it works the opposite way.

The headteachers welcome tools that differentiate between successful and failing schools. They also see OFSTED as a tool that gives them credit for their hard work. However, they have substantial reservations about the contents and methods of OFSTED, which include:

1. The lengthy preparation method for the audit allows what Stephen Ball (2003) labels a 'fabrication culture'. The headteachers are voicing a will to have unannounced flash-audits. The idea is daunting but it seems the headteachers who took part in this study are gradually forming an opinion in favour of such audits.[2] It is seen as fairer to them and to their hard-working staff.
2. The headteachers think that inspections are too heavy-handed and without enough context or culture sensitivity. The standards audited and enforced are, simply, too 'standardised'. As the system becomes increasingly diverse, the headteachers think inspection should be built further around distinct categories of schools. The categories should evolve and take into account the area (city, inner city, rural), the student population (defined in SES, free school meals, refugees, majority/ minority, etc.), physical aspects (one-site, split-site, a building under preservation laws, etc.), size, funding (community, foundation, VA/VC, grammar, comprehensive, secondary, specialist/CTC, etc.), and constraints on pupil enrolment. They also think that political aspects of education should be inspected no less than pedagogic and attainment parameters. To their mind audit is focused too much on schools and not enough on LEAs and the government itself – two bodies perceived by the headteachers as responsible for many of the system's problems.
3. The headteachers think that the system is over-inspected and under-supported or consulted. As David Nevo, a renowned expert on educational evaluation and editor of the leading journal on the subject[3] says: 'weighing one's self often, does not cause weight loss'.
4. The headteachers have to learn how to prepare for OFSTED inspections either by trial and error – and very few heads get the chance of going through more than two inspections during their tenure – or by hiring consultants and organisational psychology private firms who prepare schools for inspection, but can be expensive. Such a situation is, as the headteachers say, annoying.
5. Finally, the headteachers caution that there is very little concern among policy makers on the cultural ramifications of the audits on staff morale and daily life in schools and for teaching and learning. The head-

teachers report that inspection year is often a lost year, pedagogically, though preparation for inspection has important advantages for building the school's capacity, plans, structure, and strengthening bonds among members of the senior and middle management teams and the head-teachers.

The headteachers direct their critique not only towards OFSTED and school audit but also to the government's role as regulator. However, this opinion is not very consistent. On the one hand, they think government initiatives drive schools into unnecessary and stressful competition on unequal terms. Law-based reform strengthens some components of the system unevenly and the government *itself* competes with schools, for instance by establishing new kinds of schools that receive favourable treatment, more money, and more attention. Headteachers of foundation schools, that were the 'coming thing' only a few years ago, are now struggling to maintain their status against the appearance of specialist schools and CTCs. Headteachers of inner city secondary and compre-hensive high schools struggle against losing their sixth forms to new 16–19 colleges that are able to offer better staff and state-of-the-art laboratories, ICT, and such. Headteachers of inner city primary schools are worried when other neighbouring primaries benefit from being involved in Education Action Zones and Excellence in Cities public–private partnerships (PPPs). This latter example produces frustration also because some headteachers feel the conditions of their schools are iden-tical or even significantly *worse* than the conditions of the schools that did get into such projects. They feel that LEA politics often give unfair advantage to one school as opposed to another. This is, therefore, one side of the equation: too much uneven regulation.

On the other side of the equation, headteachers feel government does not interfere *enough* in strengthening weaker schools in weaker areas, and disregards problematic local conditions such as ailing and corrupt LEAs that cannot manage education properly. This story is therefore complicated and the message sent to law-based reform designers is not coherent. Finally, admissions policy and appeal procedures are another sub-area under the title of free market and regulation. The headteachers feel that admissions and appeals seriously hinder free market practices:

> Admissions policy is a very blunt instrument that creates unnecessary work. Schools should be able to make their own arrangements where appropriate (admissions levels – not criteria).

> Over-regulation prevents flexibility and creativity.... It seems unnecessary to have areas so strictly regulated. Why have admissions criteria at all if, after the school is full, independent appeal committees disregard them and you have to take the children; or governors interfere and force us to take in children we don't have room for? It makes a mockery of the whole process.

> Having to use money for certain things is a problem. Who knows the school best? The government or us? As a school that in recent years has attracted significantly more pupils than our standard number, we feel what is needed is for clear guidance by law, coupled with good liaison with the LEA. As a foundation school, we have our own admissions authority. We are an oversubscribed school. The admissions criteria are vague and appeals committees do not add clarity.

> There are absolutely not enough resources to handle admissions. My school has experienced an average 37 per cent pupil mobility for the last four years, so SATs are a poor measure. Funding takes minimal account of turbulence (370 children on roll, and only £6,500 added to budget to address mobility issues).

As pointed out before, headteachers welcome opening the enrolment arena to competition. But they think legal appeal requirements are often biased through local politics, and indeed limit the true 'market' aspects of the process. According to the headteachers, LEAs that oversubscribe schools without providing appropriate resources abuse the local management of schools – the same management that gave schools financial autonomy. Per-pupil funding is provided, but when additional rooms, staff, and equipment are required, it is a different story.

Another example in the legal-political sphere is the legal requirement for worship in maintained schools. Headteachers, particularly in inner city and poor neighbourhood areas, see it as a problematic issue. These schools have a large percentage of non-Christian, often non-white students. Many are refugees and many are illegal immigrants from the Caribbean, Somalia, Kosovo, Bangladesh, and other war-torn areas around the world. As the debate on immigration continues, headteachers in schools with a large number of students from these places feel the pressure. They feel that legislation on worship ignores the practicality of life in an inner city school. It alienates them and estranges their schools from mainstream English society. It demarcates legitimate culture from marginalised culture. All this is accompanied by government rhetoric on inclusion and multiculturalism. Other headteachers point out that such 'worship' is required even in schools with few or no Christian students at all. The headteachers themselves see this kind of law as situated in the midst of the legal-political domain, but it is perhaps hardly ever possible to implement it fully according to the legal requirement, regardless of means, capacity tools, etc. Solutions vary from total disregard, to having multi-religious 'worship' in separate rooms for each of the various denominations that exist among the student body, to having 'collective worship' with no Christian characteristics but just some general statements or texts that can be interpreted and accepted by everyone.

The purely legal initiatives are seen as much more straightforward and pedagogical in nature, as well as more 'aware' of life and working conditions in schools. The legal-political issues are seen as carrying a hidden political or other agenda, usually aimed at appeasing voters and constituencies at the expense of creating feasible working conditions in schools, while ignoring the day-to-day problems of headteachers and their staff. One differentiating methodology, used to decide whether a specific piece of educational legislation belongs either to the legal-political domain or to the purely legal domain is financial and supportive: when legislative mandates create substantial organisational, administrative, and therefore also budgetary burden, without adequate funds, they are tagged as 'legal-political'. When the headteachers feel the government is making *some* effort, and combines mandatory policy with at least *some* tools, support, consultancy, training, or money, they are willing to look at such legislation as 'purely legal'. The distinction between the 'legal-political' and the 'purely legal' is very important for policy makers, and is a main finding of this study, because it affects headteachers' behaviour. The headteachers report that while in the purely legal cases, their tendency is to comply with the written letter of the law, their attitude towards the legal-political is scornful and suspicious. They declare openly that they do not intend to comply with this category of legislation and feel free to circumvent, if not deliberately sabotage, policy that accompanies it. Such a disposition possibly explains why these policies will probably not be implemented, certainly not in the manner and to the extent that policy makers and law-makers have in mind. Such interpretation by headteachers is probably one of the sources for misunderstandings between headteachers and officials. When politicians and administrators depict headteachers as conservative and resistant to change and reform, they need to bear in mind findings such as this. This distinction between the legal-political and the purely legal is interesting, and probably important for policy makers and lawmakers in England.

A final note in this section relates to the role of litigation. This study is focused on law-based reform so there is no discussion of litigation, although this is certainly a concern for headteachers. They express their worries that legal aid and insurance against lawsuits are the coming thing. Typical lawsuits mentioned are about admissions, about special educational needs (SEN) statements, about violence and safety in schools, about human rights issues especially due to conflicts between English human rights laws and High Court rulings and the European Convention on Human Rights and its interpretation in the European court. It is quite clear that this area needs further exploration and will become part of headteachers' work and concern in years to come (Ford *et al.* 1999; Ruff 2002).

How law-based reform reshaped the education system

The headteachers all agree that law has reshaped the structure of England's educational system (see Figure 5.2).

Figure 5.2 *UK principals' mindscape of British educational system policy (from 2001) and their role within*

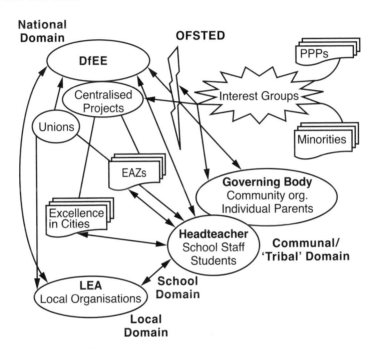

Despite massive legislation that *supposedly* organised the system several times over since the 1980s, and *supposedly* clarified distribution of power, responsibilities, and authority, the headteachers describe the outcome, in terms of structure and roles within the system, as chaotic and unstable. Moreover, it can hardly be described as hierarchic. The headteachers identify four main distinct levels, or more accurately, *domains.* First, the *national domain*, which includes, primarily, England's ministry of education (DfES), and the various government projects and initiatives. The second is the *local domain*, which consists of the local educational authority (LEA) – the city, town, or rural educational authority. The third is the *communal domain*, which consists of the immediate geographical or demographic surroundings of the school, and includes the students' parents, various parents' organisations, and the school governing body.

Finally, the fourth is the *school domain* itself, including the headteacher, the teachers, and the students. The hierarchy and relations among these four main domains, and their placement, change constantly according to the specific nature of relations that exist among all parties involved, in every school, neighbourhood, town or political/educational situation. Therefore the actual powers of the various domains are localised and individual in character, and are always the base for political power struggles, negotiations, constant building of coalitions, and identifying opposition and opportunities for action. The government, while declaring school autonomy and self-management as its major policy, anchored in legislation, circumvents its own declarations through highly centralised and aggressive government projects, coupled with OFSTED's tough audits and inspections. On top of all this, countless political, religious, ethnic, and ideological groups have an influence, attempting not only to affect the system as a whole, but also to create their own controlled, and often segregated, schools and school networks, in which these groups can determine who learns, what is taught, and who teaches. The government itself encourages this process by establishing networks of schools, and by supporting schools of faith. This leaves the majority of schools, which carry the burden of England's state education system, in a 'minority' situation. The headteachers see themselves in this model as jugglers who are often crushed under an impossible workload, created primarily by an overdose of initiatives – mandatory law-based reforms – that keep the system in a constantly fluctuating state. The headteachers see the system as 'flattened' and themselves and their schools as being at the bottom of the heap, while simultaneously the primary leaders and carriers of change, reform, and innovation. As managers of end units, they see schools as the locus of change. They see themselves as members of a professional group that has the closest connection with the stakeholders of education: the general public, the parents, and the students. This is supposed to give them an advantage over policy makers and officials. But the field of education is messy and characterised by conflict and competition – not among schools, a phenomenon generally seen as positive by the headteachers, but among the national and local authorities. This is not a good sign for policy makers. Despite all legislation, the headteachers see much of the latest policy and law as a power struggle or political game, irrelevant to the true aims of educational policy. They object to the school being turned into an arena of continuous struggle among authorities for the control of education, exacting a high price from school and headteacher as the school loses autonomy, and time and resources are diverted to manage the struggles and to juggle between the various interests.

The headteachers are, however, aware of the potential benefits of power struggle. They take advantage of the situation by making the best of all worlds. The political capabilities of headteachers in the early twenty-first century are obviously useful in this new state of things. The headteachers see the Labour government as more trustworthy and straightforward than all other groups involved. Two-thirds of headteachers are suspicious and critical towards LEAs, from seeing the LEAs as presently having no real role in education and therefore having to come up with new roles and duties that are quite artificial, to seeing them as corrupt, inefficient, and extremely wasteful. In short, LEAs are an unnecessary financial and bureaucratic headache or overhead, in an already tightly budgeted system. The headteachers fail to understand why, under the auspices of local management (LMS), they are required to receive certain professional and administrative services from the LEA instead of purchasing these services for themselves. The government, in its role as regulator, is distant and is defined in terms of good intentions – sometimes gone sour unintentionally but still coming up with some good ideas.

A major trait of educational law-based reform is the sense of stability that accompanies the relatively strict guidelines on how schools should be run and organised. The headteachers point to the fact that using primary legislation, with the wide public debate that precedes and accompanies it, allows swift establishment of totally new kinds of structures and practices, the most important being school-based management and direct funnelling of money to schools that received 'grant-maintained' status from the late 1980s. The headteachers of this type of school had considerably more power to decide on school policy. Headteachers in this study are aware that this important and (in their eyes) emancipatory change could not have been achieved without law-based reform. They also see many other changes that are related to law-based reform, such as the appearance of popular educational magazines (the most important probably being the TES but there are several others) and websites,[4] all established and encouraged by the 1980 Education Act.[5] The government's overarching 'takeover' of educational law and policy generated public interest in education, which is generally welcomed by headteachers. Being in the limelight is both intimidating and attractive, but has turned headteachers into 'mini public figures' in their immediate communities. They are certainly not middle managers at the LEA level, as they saw themselves in the past. The price for this, however, is paid in the 'currency' of stability and coherence. This important issue of educational law is being undermined, say the headteachers, by the practice of introducing new legislation every few years and constantly changing and shifting the powers handed down to school headteachers and their counterparts – LEA officials, governors, parents – throughout the system. For instance, the unique status of grant-maintained (now foundation) schools is gradually diminishing as LEA schools begin to receive similar status and funds, which of course means fewer funds for the grant-maintained. This happened only a few years after grant-maintained schools were introduced. Legislation is labelled not as promoting stability but as encouraging faddism. Paradoxically, educational law provides a clear sense of purpose and structure, while at the same time it is used for the introduction of frequent, sudden, and fashionable changes, thus causing headteachers to feel insecure and to adopt a 'pawn' rather than 'source' image. But as was shown previously, the headteachers also think that educational law has upgraded their role considerably, and they have, indeed, become leaders and social advocates within their school communities. Headteachers feel that legislation is often heavy-handed, ignores local circumstances, and is renovated and changed so often that sustainability of reform is difficult, and sometimes impossible. They also do not always accept the notion that standards and demands, which are presented to them, actually have a 'system' approach in mind, something that was found by Prestine (2000) as necessary for successful implementation of reform by school headteachers. They do feel, however, that the principles of law-based reform have their role in mind, in the sense that headteachers have indeed been given additional (if not sufficient, and not necessarily accompanied by adequate resources and capacity tools) powers and status for which they have wished for quite a while.

Primary versus secondary school headteachers: how law-based reform deals with size and age

One of the areas that trouble some of the headteachers in this study is the role of law-based reform as a divider among several groups of schools. One group is that of primary schools and secondary schools. A second group is that of small and large schools. A third group is city and town schools as opposed to rural schools. A fourth group is that of inner city schools and city schools. The last division is between schools in poor, minority, and immigrant population areas and schools in well-to-do areas (this category overlaps the third one to some extent). The headteachers see these divisions as programmatic and a bit conspirative. At best, they think law-based reform simply addresses a uniform non-existent model of school that is in the 'minds' of policy makers, perhaps part of the linear quality of educational policy (Ball 1994). At worst, this is part of a secret government plan to rid the system of small rural schools, and reduce the role of comprehensive schooling in England's system while upgrading the role of segregated or elitist institutions such as grammar schools, specialist schools, and CTCs. Headteachers are particularly angry at what they see as discrepancies between official rhetoric that engulfs and embraces all types of schools, and law-based reform that excludes and weakens certain types of schools.

The divisions between primary and secondary, and between small and large schools are similar. Primary schools and small schools are experiencing difficulties in coping with the administrative effects of LMS. Headteachers in these schools, who also have to teach, report a significant rise in their workload. These headteachers, perhaps more than their counterparts in bigger and/or secondary schools, are indeed 'headteachers' in the traditional meaning, rather than 'principals'. Before the recent reforms such headteachers were involved, for the greater part of their time and attention, in pedagogical matters. Thus they are the group that was most affected, in terms of role-change, by law-based reform. In big schools, especially secondary schools, administration and management were immanent in the headteachers' work even in its traditional, former, definition. But headteachers in small schools have enjoyed far fewer of these conditions, so for them it is a change:

> There is an increase in headteachers' workloads arising from the ERA 1988 as modified by the School Standards and Framework Act, etc. This has made the job of the small school teaching head almost impossible in terms of paperwork and time spent at work.

> There are continuous changes over a long period of time, despite promises to the contrary. It makes demands on time to read new amendments and update staff. As a teaching head in a small school, time has become scarce.

Not only do headteachers in small schools and primary schools lack resources to administer autonomy, they also lack knowledge and their schools lack the necessary administrative infrastructure. Secondary schools, and large primaries, had this infrastructure, or at least part of it, before law-based reform decentralised the system. Such infrastructures included administrators, personnel (HRM) people, and even accountants or at least book-keepers. Larger schools had much more experience in budget planning and financial control. Such schools had an obvious advantage when LMS was introduced by the early 1990s.

Strong versus weak: how law-based reform deals with social, economic, and demographic inequalities

Law-based reform is mainly criticised as an apparatus that widens socio-economic gaps among schools. The headteachers, both in weak areas *and* in well-off areas, all agree that social justice should be the government's primary concern. There are several reasons for this. First, the headteachers think the Labour government is committed, traditionally, to social justice. Second, the headteachers identify social equality as something that can be dealt with mainly at central government level. They are aware that market forces (which, as pointed out before, are generally welcome) and competition are inherently contradictory to equality and therefore they expect government, and specifically law-based reform, to balance market forces with egalitarian ones. According to the headteachers, not only does educational law fail to achieve this adequately, but it actually declares and offers legal arrangements that cause the public to *think that socio-economic gaps between poor and well-to-do areas have indeed been diminished*, or are at least being dealt with properly unlike in the past.

Stories like those of Gill, Ken, Khanum Mia, and Michael that were presented in Chapter 4, are typical of inner city schools in tough areas. The headteachers of these schools ask: for whom is law-based reform? Is it not primarily for schools, students, and teachers like their own? After all, the better-off schools in the better-off areas always manage to get by. But these headteachers feel that law-based reform in England has strengthened the strong and weakened the weak. Headteachers like Anthony, Sally, Valerie, and Dave, whose stories were presented in Chapter 3, and many other headteachers, send this strong message to Labour government as well. I keep emphasising the term 'Labour' because the headteachers underlined this title. They may expect this from any government in England, but their expectations from Labour government are much more focused. The headteachers single out law-based policies that are intended for the specific target of improving equality, such as Education Action Zones (EAZs) and Excellence in Cities. These public–private partnerships (PPPs) involve large companies in educational urban renewal projects which receive high profile and vast media coverage, partly due to widely publicised legislation. Legislation builds frameworks for these partnerships, entitlements, and types of franchises that allow the companies to take over education and later supply schools with certain services for a long period. Headteachers are doubtful as to the viability of these projects actually to make a difference, as well as suspicious that these projects lack the preliminary capabilities to make a change because they actually serve other masters, such as global mega-trends and mega-companies. Of course, these are the opinions of the headteachers who took part in this study. The opinions are of a sample of headteachers, and they are, indeed, opinions. This study has no aspirations or pretensions to study the actual effects of, for example, EAZs on attainment, truancy, socio-economic gaps, and other inequalities. Nevertheless, the opinions of headteachers on law-based reform, whether they are 'objective' or not, have immense importance for policy makers; for there is enough evidence that winning over headteachers is a basic step in any school reform.

Headteachers in well-to-do areas, especially in suburbs, work under the same laws as Gill, Ken, Khanum Mia, and Michael, but feel much better. First, they feel better *culturally*, because their population is Christian, or non-white but veteran in English society. Such populations fit in more comfortably with the mainstream mandatory programmes. Second, rather trivially, they feel better *financially*, because the parents can set up trust funds for the school, thus allowing development and major renovations, rendering them free from the grip of finance companies that some schools, such as Gill's, are forced to employ. Although all eight schools in chapters 3 and 4 are state financed ('maintained', is the legal term) and controlled, the differences between the first four and the latter are striking. The target of law-based reform has therefore been missed by a wide margin. Not all headteachers in this study imply that the government's credit on this issue is wasted or gone, but it is a note of warning.

Headteachers are concerned that the law should offer clear and manageable tools for differentiating between schools in poor areas, and schools in well-to-do areas, and for differentiating between local authorities that have (and spend) more money on schooling and others that do not. The headteachers feel the law disregards these differences. It is not that the government does not offer some solutions, such as Education Action Zones and the Excellence in Cities initiatives. Headteachers are offended by the fact that with so much legislation the status of inner city schools is not addressed formally, with all the declarative public force of law –

and presented as a national problem that requires national attention and some affirmative action. Also, the headteachers feel educational law does not address socio-political issues such as multiculturalism and its profound effect on life in many schools. The headteachers point out that multicultural issues have to be addressed on a national level or else minority and immigrant groups might be railroaded into the existing mainstream English culture. Another issue that, according to the headteachers, should to be addressed by the law, is the issue of integration (desegregation is the US term). The headteachers believe that dealing with these issues by the law would produce the means that are necessary to promote them. They welcome the legislation that puts a cap on permanent expulsions and monitors retention and truancy. But they identify a substantial gap between rhetoric on marginalisation and exclusion, and their manifestation in law-based reform.

Another group of schools that headteachers feel are marginalised by law-based reform are rural schools. Such schools tend to be small and remote so everything written here so far on school size, is relevant to their headteachers as well. In addition, there is a feeling that government initiatives focus on big cities and perceives headteachers of rural schools as a type of diminishing backwater population. The ongoing argument between Labour government and rural interest groups (such as the Countryside Alliance), which became quite heated in 2001 and 2002, also contributed to this feeling. It seems this population of headteachers, which possibly does not cater to a very large student population, but is distinct and serves quite a few schools, deserves some more targeted research on their unique conditions and problems of management and leadership.

Governing bodies and headteachers

According to the headteachers in this study, governing bodies are a major issue under law-based reform. Governing bodies are a relatively new tier in the education system. Other law-based reform strengthens or weakens existing tiers like LEAs or the DfES. The change brought with the introduction of governing bodies was swift and meaningful; within a few years governing bodies became, for better or worse, an important factor in headteachers' daily life in schools. Judging by the views of head-teachers in this study, so far this has not been a big success. At best, the work put in by the headteacher and his or her management team in 'nur-turing' the governing body, is matched by the help the governors give in defending the school, raising money, and promoting school policy. This would be in about one-third of cases, especially in affluent schools. Two-thirds of the heads have very few good things to say about governing bodies. Here are some typical statements:

> I spend an immense amount of time having to work with inadequate governors. As volunteers, they have no real understanding of the com-plexities of running a school. The level of bureaucracy prevents many willing people from taking on the role – the amount of reading required is a real problem in an area of high levels of adult illiteracy. My governing body is dominated by elderly people who feel they are helping the community by turning up at formal meetings three times a year.

> The calibre of the governors that I work with make my job harder than it need be. We need governors who are willing and able to come into school regularly, but who truly understand that their role is not to inspect the school but to support it. I feel that my chair of governors sees his role in trying to catch me out by speaking to staff. This offends all of us. Professional paid governors or willing parents and less bureaucracy would be preferable.

> I spend a lot of time explaining matters to governors, as they are not professionals in education. With so many changes, this is very time consuming despite training programmes. It is difficult to get good governors when the work is voluntary and the workload is huge.

> The involvement and responsibilities of governors and the need to ensure they are aware of what they must do is worrying. Governors are employed outside education so there is no time to update them and to ensure they know what their responsibilities are. I feel there is a lack of awareness of the implications of the job and about what the recent changes bring against a background of raising standards. The pulls are

to many different directions. Many important decisions cannot be made without a meeting of volunteers, which holds up procedures. There are too many committees and much more should be delegated to the chair and head.

Several points arise from these statements. The first point is the added, uncompensated workload especially for headteachers, but also for some senior staff. This includes writing and presenting reports to the governors, taking part in numerous meetings, and setting up the structure: searching for suitable governors, allocating roles such as membership and chairs of committees, etc. The second point is the growing involvement of the governors within the school – their relations with senior staff and teachers, with students' parents, etc. The headteachers have to set boundaries for the governors as to how far, on what issues, and with whom they can get involved in the school. On the one hand, it is clear they are responsible for the school and therefore need to be informed. On the other hand, the headteacher is worried that his or her authority might be hampered, that is, the governors might interfere in and even disturb the school's smooth operation. The third point is the conflict between the headteacher being subordinate to the governing body, according to law, and the fact that in practice the governors are lost without the coaching and guidance of the headteacher. The current consultancy possibilities offered by government are far from sufficient. The fourth point, not disconnected from the third, is the problem of actually locating suitable governors – a problem that is self-evident in weak schools in tough areas. The fifth point is the need to balance between the governing body and two important domains: the LEA and the students' parents.

The headteachers are concerned that the governing bodies do not necessarily serve the school and might become an additional supervising tier that allows the LEA further intervention and involvement in schools, thus derailing headteachers' autonomy. Although empirically, legislation is quite clear on the responsibilities of governing bodies, it is vague on their placement in the system as a whole. From studying the law, it is evident what Parliament had in mind. By stating that 'each maintained school shall have a governing body' (SSFA 1998 s. 36), Parliament established that *the governing body is part of the school*, but this intent seems not to have been fully understood by headteachers and perhaps their empirical experience with governing bodies does not support this intent either. The headteachers think governing bodies are, at least to some extent, some type of an intermediate level between LEAs and schools. They are seen as a burden that strengthens only some schools, sporadically and randomly, with strong correlation to socio-economic conditions in the school and its environment. The bottom line is, therefore, that according to the headteachers in this study, governing bodies have not yet substantiated and justified their status as a beneficial apparatus for headship and for their schools' community.

The second population that the headteachers are concerned with in regard to governing bodies is the students' parents. Before governing bodies became a big issue, the immediate and natural 'constituency' or 'stakeholders' of the headteacher and the school were the students' parents. Governing bodies upset this balance. On the one hand, the governing bodies became a powerful representative of parents' interests especially on issues like admissions and permanent exclusions. On the other hand, the headteachers feel that governing bodies are not a formal alternative for individual families and parents' rights. Sometimes the headteachers think their responsibility is to protect parents and students from governing bodies – for instance, when the latter want to rid the school of problematic children. The headteachers are torn between their responsibility to keep the school safe for the whole student body, and their awareness, at the same time, that exclusion is a severe measure for the individual student, whose behaviour might be the result of mitigating socio-economic circumstances. The governing body does not come instead of the parents but rather in addition to them, adding pressure and politics to the headteachers' already overburdened reality:

> The increase in the rights of parents to have a say in education of their children, although broadly desirable, had resulted in many schools facing pressure to justify their actions. The responsibility of the parents to make positive contributions to this process need to be far more clearly defined and promulgated by government.

I cannot, and will not, refer parents to the governing body. I feel parents have the right to negotiate directly with the headteacher. Even when the governing body decides something in regard to parents' rights in general, or about school policy towards a specific group of students or parents, I don't think that I, as headteacher, can hide behind the governing bodies. In this sense governing bodies have not changed anything – and if they have they add complexity and ambiguity.

Headteachers between the pedagogic, managerial, political, and legal spheres: handling the bureaucracy of pedagogy

The headteachers all agree that educational law shapes their role and has profound influence on leadership. They find themselves among four spheres. The first sphere is pedagogic: part of the headteachers' past role that is still evident, especially among primary school headteachers. Under this heading, they have to lead and organise a teaching–learning environment. The second sphere is managerial: headteachers have to devote more and more of their attention to their role as managers – organising the school, strategic planning, finance, human resources, and so on. The third sphere is political: forming coalitions, negotiating terms and arrangements with governing bodies, LEAs, parents, and other components of the system. The fourth sphere is legal: understanding the endless list of statutory instruments, their relations to each other, their hierarchy within the legal world, and their implications for pedagogy and management.

Contrary to the past, building and controlling this environment is overshadowed by centralised National Curriculum, Key Stages, Numeracy and Literacy policy and other standardised testing and measurement of several kinds. It is interesting that among all components of law-based reform, the National Curriculum is the one that came up as most significant in headteachers' work, although it was one of the earliest (established in the 1988 Education Reform Act). Here are some headteachers' statements:

Workload is the key issue since changes in KS4 and KS3 mean time and burden, cost for staff, and especially cost for setting up new courses so the degree of freedom is lost. League tables get teachers teaching for the test. Thus, 80 per cent of annual expenditure is determined by a structure over which we have no control. Guidance for implementation is prescriptive.

Although we have some flexibility, we cannot deviate too far from national guidance.

The National Curriculum is very prescriptive. There is little opportunity to vary content.

Headteachers paint a picture that includes several forces. One force is the National Curriculum that puts enormous constraints on headteachers and teachers' work and workload. This is followed by bureaucratic and administrative requirements that include detailed planning, documentation, and reporting. Sufficient, or even minimal, training and resources do not accompany all this. The headteachers see a connection between the bureaucracy of pedagogy and staffing:

We received a lot of paper to read (which has changed and altered almost immediately) but little else. The staffing needed to implement the reforms was generally insufficient and caused many stresses and strains. *The current problems of recruitment and retention all stem from this, in my opinion.* Revising the statutory curriculum entitlement for pupils is essential. More recently extra funding and resources have been made available. But there are too many changes to tackle too quickly, without sufficient time for reflection and consultation. (Author's emphasis.)

Headteachers caution that law-based reform operates on a managerial timetable that is considerably shorter than the pedagogic timetable. This feeling is common to headteachers in large and secondary schools, who are used to devoting much of their time to administration, rather than to pedagogy. When such headteachers speak of the National Curriculum constraints, they often refer to teachers' payment, and the relatively new law-based policy of Performance Management:

Capability procedures and the performance management process have become very important: professional development has been highlighted by this process, which can only support the aims of every school to enhance pupil learning. What is taught, emphasis on subjects, pressures to be led by statistics, higher accountability – all this enables consistency and progression and benchmarking of achievement.

Generally speaking, we have been given a huge amount of additional resources over the past four years to support the curriculum in certain key areas. But this money also influences our autonomy. There are many school aims that are hampered by this. School emphasis on economy-led foci leaves us to struggle to maintain other areas of human development like arts, etc.

The headteachers see Performance Management as a policy intended for advancing centralised curricular policy, as the following statements emphasise:

Performance Management gives a framework for staff development and narrows focus for school development: much training has been given – some good, some bad, some contradictory. Money to support implementation was insufficient to pay for adequate release time from the classroom for teachers and team leaders. Staff feel quite bewildered about what they have to teach within each term. They are so conscious of covering the curriculum that there is a definite feeling of 'loss of fun' for the children. I need time for instruction, training is needed first, then implementation – it had happened the other way round. There is a great deal of prescription on how to teach in both areas. There are ever more published tables or allegedly comparable results. (Author's emphasis.)

There are enormous constraints on what to teach. What happened to all the wonderful work done with students in lower academic abilities? Teachers' payment schemes restrict flexible approach to learning.

The extent of coverage for students – resources and training didn't follow from or precede the legal requirements. It's a wrong way to do things. It's not so easy to replace staff that is not coping with pressure: litigation, tribunals, accusations, bad feelings which are investigated whether or not they are true. Heads have little power to act quickly and are vulnerable.

Mistakes can result in sacking but there is no legal or financial training
– though there is some LEA and other support.

One could criticise the headteachers for complaining too much – whatever the government policy may be. In a way, this is true. However, these
statements by the headteachers prove, in my opinion, the enigmatic and
puzzling situation in which they find themselves. They want autonomy
and are proud of the managerial and leadership qualities of their changing
role. When the government directs and sets aside funds for specific policies,
often mandated by law, the headteachers complain that their autonomy is
decreased. When budget is agglomerated, headteachers complain the
'budget neutral' policy drains their resources. In short, a real conflict:

> Legislation that enforces schools to produce documents for parents,
> governors, LEA, DfEE is time consuming and not cost effective.
> Administrative decrees distract schools from the main purpose to
> provide education for children. It's an industry of publications and con-
> sultants. For instance, there is very little proper research to validate the
> basis of the literacy hour. Missing is respect. History tells us that inter-
> vention of the state to this extent creates massive bureaucracy and
> unreliable results. The reforms, like the introduction of the National
> Curriculum, matched the aims of our school, but the means, tools, and
> resources provided were insufficient.

The other major law-based reform from the 1980s (mandated under the
1980 Education Act) is school choice, which has been accepted by headteachers much more readily. If at all, they criticise the fact that such
choice is not more open, and constraint-free, as seen in their comments
on admissions policy, appeal procedures, and catchment areas.

Conclusion: Labour law-based reform as the last resort for headteachers

The important bottom line of this chapter is that despite their concern and
criticism towards law-based reform, headteachers are:

1. Convinced that decentralisation processes including LMS are an inseparable part of their work, and are phenomena that have changed headship and leadership profoundly – generally for the better;
2. Grateful for the balancing centralised attempts made by the Labour government since 1997 to strengthen marginalised groups of schools and to provide more equitable conditions for work. Having said that, they think government should do much more in this department, and reduce the margin between statements and action. Law-based reform is the primary tool for government to achieve these goals.

6 English law-based reform: harnessing educational leadership to reclaim public education

This chapter attempts to put together the findings on law-based reform, with the findings from the schools and the schools' headteachers. It offers some conceptual remarks and some practical ideas on the utilisation of law-based reform in England, in order to improve the work and working conditions of headteachers. As in Chapter 1, the viewpoint on law-based reform and leadership in this chapter is comparative and presents research for the UK and other countries, especially the United States.

Why has English law-based reform failed to encompass headteachers and educational leadership? Apparently, there are several reasons. One possibility is that policy makers perceive headteachers as an obstruction, a hurdle, placed in the path of school reform; they are sceptical about whether headteachers can take charge, let alone lead, the reforms. This is not a critique of English law-based reform. Findings show it is a common mistake in other countries as well (Gibton *et al.* 2000; Heubert 1999b). Or, in contrast, perhaps the reason is that authorities have faith in head-teachers' ability to adapt and comply. Or, perhaps by adopting a linear approach, lawmakers naturally assume that mandates will create the necessary conditions for change not only in structures and contents, but also in values, leadership styles, and management.

The chapter begins with some remarks on the environment that law-based reform has created for headteachers, in terms of types of schools, and models of governance. Then law-based reform is analysed in terms of what it does to public education and equality in England, again with implications for headship. Further, the changes in the role of headteachers – from pedagogy to management – are explored. Finally, the chapter offers some ideas for new balancing legislation on leadership and the system's structure.

The environment of school leadership in post-2000 England

Judging by the contents of law-based reform, the ideological roots of educational responsibility in England are not clear. Conceptually, there are three approaches to this issue, as presented in Figure 6.1. The first approach, on the left-hand side, the liberal approach backs the legal-educational doctrine of *in loco parentis* (Boyd 2004; Hyams 1997). According to this doctrine, the right and obligation for educating children rests with their parents. The liberal state is defined negatively. Its duty is to avoid interference in the life of its citizens. The liberal state interferes only when one citizen inflicts damage – in its strictest sense, physical or financial – on another. The liberal doctrine (Brown 1986; Rawls 1971; Strike 2004) is embedded in the work of nineteenth-century philosophers like John Stuart Mill ([1859], 1977). *In loco parentis* means that powers of the parents are transferred to the school, which serves as their 'extended arm'. The second approach is collective. As seen in the middle of Figure 6.1, it is best described by the concept of the 'social contract' and the work of French philosopher Rousseau. This approach assumes that the provider and controller of education is society as a whole, anchored in the power of the state. The state expropriates the powers of education from individual parents because it views education as a public asset, destined for the public's good. The third approach is 'tribal' or 'parochial', on the right-hand side of the model, and sees education as the property and responsibility of factions and groups *within* the democratic state. Such factions, that have a religious, ethnic, gender, or political denomination, want to have their own schools in which they may exercise control over who teaches, who learns, and what is taught. This ideology characterises a postmodern society (Bottery 2000; Boyd 2004; Hargreaves 1995). Does law-based reform in England solve the contradictions among these ideologies? According to headteachers and according to the law, the answer is no.

The world of educational leaders in post-2000 England is decentralised and diverse. It is legally saturated. During the past two decades of law-based reform, an English headteacher is likely to have encountered two major law-based reforms during his or her tenure as head, plus several

Figure 6.1 *The source of educational authority*

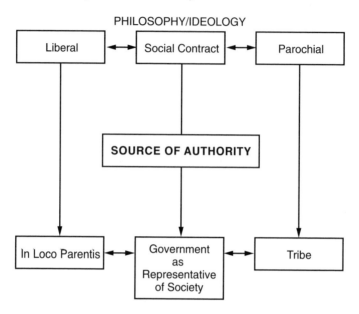

mini-reforms that are far from being insignificant. In a short period, these reforms have changed the landscape of English education. Figure 6.2 depicts one of the most important aspects of these reforms – the resegregation of England's school system.

This change reflects the government's move away, structurally, politically, and socially, from comprehensive education. Paradoxically, while introducing choice as a main component of school reform, under the Conservative government comprehensive high schools were strengthened. Although schools were never really integrated in the US sense,[1] comprehensive schooling was still an important statement. The Labour government from 1997, allowed, built, and encouraged new and existing types of schools that focused on certain types of students, of curriculum, or of faith, or all together. Even grant-maintained (now foundation) schools (an English version of charter schools, as they are called in the US and Canada), were never used for ideological – e.g. religious – or ethnic alternatives from mainstream English education. This form of educational

Figure 6.2 *England's decentralised school system post 2000*

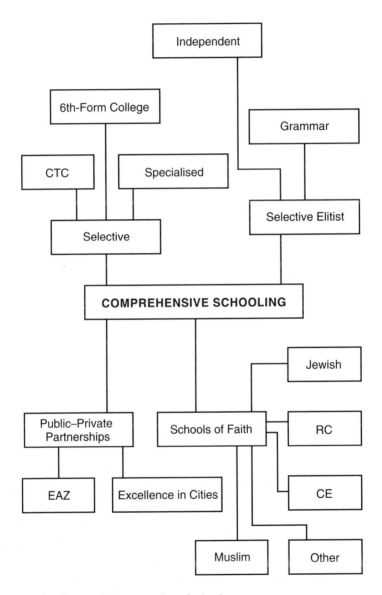

Note: Box size does not indicate number of schools.

organisation was an administrative and financial, rather than cultural or religious, change. Under Labour, although community schools and foundation schools are still the vast majority of England's public[2] education system, new types of schools are appearing in large numbers and becoming popular and – what is more important – legitimate in the eyes of the public. This is a benchmark when discussing the fate of English public education – an issue that will be discussed later in this chapter.

Such findings coincide with US research on headteachers whose systems have gone through similar decentralisation and restructuring processes, both on the empowering (Goldring and Rallis 1993; Goldring and Greenfield 2002; Seashore-Louis and Murphy 1994) and the bewildering sides (Hallinger and Hausman 1994; Wildy and Louden 2000), even in much less legislated environments than England's. What is common to such reforms is a will to re-evaluate boundaries and definitions that produce ongoing dilemmas, i.e. clashes between 'durable value conflicts' (Goldring and Greenfield 2002: 12; Ogawa *et al.* 1999). The values are manageable but 'not resolvable'. Typical dilemmas can occur between excellence and equity; or between mainstream basic knowledge and multiculturalism. Law-based reform in England has not lessened the conflicts these dilemmas present to headteachers. Declarations of politicians, strategy papers, Green Papers, White Papers, and other documents created an atmosphere of hope that government was taking control over the dilemmas and was offering clear priorities. This hope has not been fulfilled; rather, law-based reform has added tension and ambiguity. Problems of ambiguity also come from what Goldring and Greenfield (2002: 8–9) refer to as 'hybrid governance', or what Hill (2004: 77) calls a 'diverse provider' model. This means that numerous agencies attempt to control schools and influence what goes on in them. In this situation schools turn into battle grounds for control of educational 'turf' – battles in which headteachers and schools in general quickly become victims. The conclusion of this study is that law-based reform has not helped in clearing up this ambiguity. In fact, the ambiguity has grown worse, when compared to Conservative law-based reform. The latter is criticised by the headteachers from many aspects, but in a way was more clear in its structure and in what it attempted to gain. From 1997, reforms have attempted to empower schools, but strengthen LEAs; then they attempted to weaken LEAs and strengthen parents; then to empower governing bodies and strengthen parents; then again to strengthen headteachers and strengthen governing bodies; then to allow more autonomy but retake education by central government; and so on. Contradicting and clashing initiatives and structures amaze headteachers and induce a sense of insecurity, temporality, and estrangement. In the end, why should the headteacher comply – it will all change quite soon, anyway. This feeling is not only problematic for headteachers – it is dangerous for reform. According to Prestine (2000), when headteachers feel reforms do not last and structure is fluid, they ignore reforms and simply get on with their job.

Table 6.1 presents an analysis and summary of headteachers' views on how law-based reform works in strengthening and weakening strong schools or strengthening and weakening schools in weak areas with Glatter's (2002) models of governance. The table shows that law-based reform has two major flaws. The first flaw is inconsistency in the current model of governance. The table shows nearly equal dispersal among the four models that Glatter defines – disregarding the conflicts and tensions between them. This situation possibly adds to ambiguity and confusion among headteachers. It also shows that law-based reform, and perhaps the government behind it, is either truly inconsistent or simply unaware of the implications that its policy has on the system's governance. The second flaw is it seems that law-based reform has not succeeded in disconnecting the link between central government policies and the widening gaps between schools in strong areas and schools in weak areas – a target that, according both to Labour government and to the headteachers, is central to government's targets and headteachers' moral belief. The government, despite its declarations – which, it is important to highlight, are perceived as sincere by the headteachers – fails to create conditions for schools in weak areas to compete with schools in strong areas, or to enable them to extricate themselves from the problematic situation in which they feel entrenched. Except for Education Action Zones and Excellence in Cities – which are not ignored, but limited, and have their

Table 6.1 *How law-based reform influences schools in strong and weak areas, using Glatter's (2002) models of governance*

Categories	Glatter's models of governance			
	CM: competitive market	SE: school empowerment	LE: local empowerment	QC: quality control
Empowering heads vs. DfES	@@@@@	@@@@@	@@@@ ###	@@@ ##
Weakening heads vs. DfES	###	####		###
Empowering heads vs. LEA	@@@@@	@@@@@ ####		@@@@@ ###
Weakening heads vs. LEA	###		@@@@@ ####	
Empowering heads vs. school governing body	@@@@ #####	@@@@@		
Weakening heads vs. school governing body		####	@@@ ###	
Empowering heads vs. school staff	@@@@@ ###	@@@@@ #####		@@@@@
Weakening heads vs. school staff			@@@ ####	##
Empowering heads vs. pupils' parents		###		@@@@@
Weakening heads vs. pupils' parents	@@@@ ###	@@@	@@ #	##

Notes: @: school in strong area; #: school in weak area.

problems – the models of governance advanced by law-based reform work in favour of schools in strong areas. While attempting to improve the situations for schools in inner cities and weaker areas, the government itself competes with these schools, not only by creating conditions in favour of stronger schools, but also by establishing and promoting selective and elitist government-financed schools (Gewirtz 1998; Gillborn 1998; Gillborn and Youdell 2000; Levacic *et al.* 2003; Whitty *et al.* 1998). These include: grammar schools, whether single-sex or co-educational, which can select their students from a large area and offer them a better government-financed head start; specialist schools and CTCs, which attract good students and receive more money and better conditions in return for a vague commitment to coach other schools; and schools of faith that openly use religion as a segregational tool to sort and classify students. Unfortunately, 'there is no convincing evidence to date that the provision of notional choices of other schools provides a realistic alternative solution' (Whitty *et al.* 1998: 124). This means that free market practices have not succeeded in creating better conditions for the population in weaker areas, including minority groups, immigrants, and refugees. Government intervention, probably through law-based reform, is critical for improving the 'deal' these groups receive from English society.

Moving on from the general socio-economic conditions within which headteachers operate, to the issue of accountability, Table 6.2 compares between a list of themes that Adams and Kirst (1999) see as necessary for accountability mechanisms to work properly, and findings from the headteachers in this study.

Out of 14 themes, law-based reform achieves only five to a full extent. Three out of five are about indicators, about accounts, and about rewards or sanctions. They are important, but they tend to be the themes that can be accomplished first, and often solely (Hannaway 2004). Four themes received 'low' or 'non-existent' grades. Yet, these are considered to be the most important themes for achieving accountability among 'agents' i.e. headteachers. They are about clear definitions of principals and agents, about conflict between design elements, about adequate resources for compliance, and about causal responsibility.

Table 6.2 *Themes of accountability mechanisms according to Adams and Kirst (1999) and their manifestation in English law-based reform*

Theme	English law-based reform
Clear definition of principals and agents	Quite unclear. Except for the DfES, which is clearly the principal, all other players are both principals *and* agents, sometimes simultaneously.
Adequate authorisation to focus agent's actions	Responsibilities and authorities of the DfES, LEAs, school governing bodies, and headteachers are also unclear and tend to overlap without clear boundaries.
Consistency between work context and accountability goals	Not always. Bureaucratic control is meshed into typical professional and pedagogical issues in areas like exclusions and performance management.
Conflicts between design elements	Quite common. For instance, drive for inclusivity clashes with segregative types of schools such as grammar schools, specialist schools, etc. Zero-tolerance policy on bullying and violence clash with retention policy. Christian worship clashes with multiculturalism.
Well-defined accounts, using meaningful, valid, and reliable data	Not quite. Long and accumulating lists of responsibilities. Some accounts are clear through OFSTED inspections, league tables, and PANDAs.
Useful indicators for principals and agents	Yes – it seems both authorities and headteachers have useful indicators now: dropout rates, five A–Cs, Key Stages 1–5, numeracy and literacy indicators, etc.
Accounts can judge schools	Yes – it seems accounts can judge schools on some important parameters.
Accountability sufficient for rewards and sanctions	Probably on the sanctions end – OFSTED inspections, special measures, and school closure; as for rewards, published results promote successful schools. However, it seems these instruments are not always delicate and accurate enough.
Agent's discretion	Partial – detailed regulations and bureaucratic constraints on exclusion issues, performance management, and governing bodies regulations.

Table 6.2 *continued*

Theme	English law-based reform
Agent's resources	Most problematic. Substantial advantages for VA/VC schools, schools in better-off areas with more LEA money or trust funds, some balance for schools in weaker areas due to EAZ/Excellence in Cities areas. Teacher recruitment problems in many areas.
Agent's acting capability	Leadership is very important, and so are school-based initiatives, but surrounding outer circumstances have immense influence on capabilities.
Is there principal support?	Generally yes – there is a sense of support, although also coupled with a sense of abandonment, especially in inner city schools.
Commensurability of sanctions and causal responsibility	Hardly. Schools and headteachers are held totally responsible. External variables are vague and not taken into account. If they are the criteria, they are not clear.
Incentives that motivate agents	Partly – perhaps their tenure as headteachers and their school's survival. Perhaps enrolling better students. Sometimes receiving different status such as specialist, etc. but there is a strong sense of contingency among headteachers.

Source: Themes are based on Adams and Kirst (1999: 480).
Notes: Dark grey: very low or non-existent; light grey: partial implementation; white: compliance with theme.
The term 'principal' is used as in principal-agent organisational theory, not to be confused with principal as US for headteacher.

Studies on the conditions required for the success of centralised school reform and the work of educational leaders (Glatter 2003; Hannaway 2004; Leithwood *et al.* 1999; Mehan *et al.* 2003; Prestine 2000) suggest several important factors. These include a sense of the authenticity of the reform, special care for the importance of local context and cultural characteristics, building genuine partnerships, reducing the impact of a 'high-stakes' environment, and building true trust among educational leaders, together with the need to sustain reform over long periods of time (Hargreaves and Fink 2003), and the need to ensure that the normative and cultural rational of reform is clear and assimilated down the line from policy makers to policy implementers (Glatter 2003; Mehan *et al.* 2003; Prestine 2000; Vogel *et al.* 2002). Not all of these are evident in England's law-based reform.

The crisis of public education, law-based reform, educational leadership, and implications for social justice

English law-based reform under the Labour government certainly constitutes a serious attempt to confront the problems of public education, which is under serious attack (Boyd 2004; Cibulka 2004; Hannaway 2004; Hill 2004; Kirst 2004; Linn 2003; Lubienski 2002; Miron and Nelson 2002; Strike 2004). The stories of headteachers in this study are, in more than one way, not only the stories of educational leadership, but also the story of the struggle to preserve public education in England and in other English-speaking Anglo-American ethos-based nations. Lubienski (2002) explains that public education has entered a new phase in the 1990s and in the new millennium:

> An area such as education necessarily involves competing goals ... and visions ... that necessarily conflict in a pluralistic society. Therefore public education is inherently politicised. Efforts to de-politicise schooling by encouraging individuals to pursue only his or her vision as an end – while, at first glance, enticing as a neat and conflict-free alternative to messy and conflict-ridden political processes – neglect the prior interest and claim that each member of society has in and on the education of others.
>
> (Lubienski 2002: 25)

Lubienski's important contribution to the understanding of what public education is, became, and ought to be, is this: while in the past, public education enforced the public interest in education, it now represents merely the investment of public funds. Many groups that comprise the 'public' see public education as a kind of trade-off. In return for much greater freedom in influencing the education of one's own children, members of the public have given up their franchise to influence what type, arrangements, and content of education is provided for someone else's child. This 'new deal' is especially appealing to three groups that have accumulated considerable political and social influence in the last two decades. One group includes those calling for multicultural education and especially those who flinch from any type of mainstream education and want the school to strengthen cultural roots of all kinds. The second group includes upper classes that aspire to a segregated, elitist education that will enable their children to retain their social status. A third group includes middle-class families that want their children to achieve higher SES than their own, and believe free market, choice, and managerialist practices borrowed from the business world can help gain this goal, with less, or at least more cost-effective, public expense. This last group is especially concerned with public education, which is being financed by their taxes, but is quite free from public control over the basic processes of 'production' (Bottery 2000). Although there are disagreements and conflicts of interest among these groups they 'unite', even for a short while, to push forward this new interpretation of what public education is and how it should work. William Boyd (2004) has written a powerful chapter on public education, which he entitles 'a religion'. Traditionally, this 'religion' includes:

> The ideology of the governance of public schools is deeply committed to a belief in a democratic system of 'common' public schools, operated as well as financed by the government, that provides standardised curriculum, treats everyone equally (irrespective of social class, culture, race or religion) and is accountable to a publicly elected school board. As part of a non-profit public organisation, schools are (ideally) supposed to be insulated from both politics and competition. They should not compete with one another for students or resources, or use selective or 'elitist' admission policies ... this makes 'magnet' schools, charter schools, and other departures from the norm problematic.
>
> (Boyd 2004: 5)

These last types of schools, that appeared in England as well in a 'glocalised' version (see Figure 6.2), represent what Boyd sees as

> A paradigm shift in public education ... marked by a change in focus from inputs *to* the system to the outcomes and accountability *of* the system; by a shift in the attitudes of key constituency groups; and by a critical reexamination of what public education means and how it can or should be delivered.
>
> (Boyd 2004: 7, emphases in the original)

The neo-conservative new-right influence on, and critique of, public education, enhanced these processes considerably again, not only in the US (Boyd 2004) but also in England (Whitty *et al.* 1998). This paradox is what headteachers confront: the change is not from a just system to an unjust system. It is from one unjust SES-laden, social-preservation-based class system to a competitive market-controlled, often superficial system that is still heavily class-oriented, exclusive, marginalising, and culturally biased, which falsely represents a new approach to the equitable targets of public education (Gewirtz 1998; Gillborn and Youdell 2000). The new forces of accountability, choice, and standardised supervision give the public a notion, to quote one headteacher, that: 'The public feels "at last we have the buggers running".' This comment reflects a strong sense of 'settling the score', which often turns into a gloomy reality of 'more of the same'.

The headteachers in this study, who were found to be highly committed to social justice and fair distribution of social goods, find this new deal of public education puzzling. What exactly should they be? Conservative masters of the schools committed to England's old class system? (Probably not.) Neo-Marxist suspicious revolutionaries who see government conspiracies meant to appease the masses, while retaining power for old and new elite groups? (Perhaps, a bit.) Managerial business bottom-line specialists who run an efficient and successful 'shop'? (Perhaps, quite a bit.) Communal leaders who assist a bewildered community in bringing up children for tomorrow's globalised, borderless, sophisticated and ever-changing world, while retaining human dignity, compassion, and fairness as much as possible and keeping an open eye for national educational policy? (Bingo!) The last point deserves some more detail. Research shows that headteachers' roles have indeed changed towards their becoming local, non-political leaders who have a responsibility to their community, and not just to the student body and students' parents (Goldring *et al.* 2002). Findings also show the importance of having headteachers understand national policy and law-based reform (Gibton *et al.* 2000; Goldring and Rallis 1993; Prestine 2000). In our study (Gibton *et al.* 2000) of 50 headteachers of 'autonomous' schools (a softer, 1990s Israeli version of foundation schools), we found that headteachers of these relatively advanced schools have a good national viewpoint. They need such a viewpoint: first, in order to fulfil their local and communal role sufficiently; and second, because their moral role cannot be achieved without a national viewpoint in mind. For instance, if government wants to achieve integration, it needs the assistance of headteachers in affluent communities. Such headteachers might, if they only have a local agenda, apply 'commando' tactics to circumvent government egalitarian law-based policy and rid the school of children from weaker areas. For instance, in our study we found headteachers of primary schools in some of the richest neighbourhoods who went to a great effort, including some confrontation with parents, to bring in students with SEN statements from other areas of the city, as part of their view that such action has important policy ramifications on a national scale. Therefore, planners have to think how to harness headteachers to national policy and make sure each headteacher is the local representative of law-based reform. To assure this, headteachers have to be partners of reform, and have to understand what is going on, even in a large state like England with many thousands of schools.

The elusive quality of law-based reform in England, as determined in this study, and in the United States (DeMitchell and Fossey 1997; Heubert 1999b; Orfield 1999; McUsic 1999; Weckstein 1999; Welner 2000) is difficult for headteachers. There is an extremely thin line between choice as a liberal mechanism of freedom and the bulldozing quality of capitalist inequality. There is a thin line between the need for stewardship

(Goldring and Greenfield 2002) and accountability, in the sense of providing the public with real value for its taxes, and a hidden agenda of shifting the weaker students around to weaker schools in order to improve attainment in strong schools. Law-based reform plays a crucial role in determining on which side of these lines the school and its headteacher are and will be situated in the near future. Levacic *et al.* (2003) show how policy in one county consistently strengthens strong grammar schools over upper schools. This is done through unequal funding and choice (by providing free transport for grammar school students and paid transport for semi-comprehensive upper school students). It creates a fundamentally unequal system under the law that sends a clear message of exclusion and limited social prospects to many headteachers, staff, parents, and students.

The demand for deeper and longstanding parent involvement in schools and forming communities (McGaughy 2000; Sergiovanni 1994; Smrekar 1996) is contradicted by the danger that social capital eventually becomes the divider among schools (Smrekar 1996). There is evidence that law-based reform contributes to the widening of these gaps, based on differences in cultural capital (Booth and Bussell 1999). It is unintentional, but nevertheless disturbing. This is another area where educational leadership and headteachers can and do step in. It is very difficult to control the formation and implementation of parent involvement practices from afar. Headteachers are closer and can help to balance, at least to some extent, the interests between local political powers, cultural capital, and children's rights in schools. Of course, legislation that assists headteachers in this quest is very important and useful. Law-based reform is needed to balance the conflictual demands of the public in a postmodern society. Mitchell and Encarnation (1984) outline four basic demands. The first is fairness achieved through desegregation, equal funding, etc. The second is excellence, achieved through high-standard programmes, elitist and selective streaming and schooling. The third demand is choice and variety achieved by offering the public new curricula, new types of schools that provide for the students' qualifications, needs, gifts, etc. The fourth demand is cost-effectiveness, which means spending as little public funds as possible.

The role of law-based reform is to provide reasonable frameworks for headteachers to assist them in reducing the contradictions among these demands that concern schools and their heads.

One of the most evident and disturbing conflicts that law-based reform has created for the headteachers is that of accountability, market-based competition, excellence, and managerialist principles versus egalitarianism, narrowing socio-economic and ethnic gaps, and equality. Literature, both sociological (Gewirtz 1998; Gillborn and Youdell 2000; Whitty *et al.* 1998) and law-review type (Harris 2000; Monk 1997) caution about this conflict. As presented in Figure 1.2, the restructuring process of systems and schools is a two-force model that is drifting apart. This study shows that law-based reform has not cleared the ambiguity – but actually enhanced it. The law itself has established processes and mechanisms that endanger equality. Gillborn and Youdell (2000) in their powerful study of educational policy in England, agree:

> Our argument is that schools are rationing education ... our analysis suggests that this situation has worsened regardless of the political party in government; despite the rhetoric of inclusivity and empowerment; and irrespective of the motivation of pupils. The British school system is increasingly selective, disciplinary and discriminatory.
>
> (Gillborn and Youdell 2000: 1)

Of course, the English school system was not egalitarian before the new policies were introduced in the first wave of law-based reform under the Conservative government in the 1980s and the second wave under the Labour government from the later 1990s. So perhaps any change is for the better.

Between pedagogy and managerialism: headship in role change and moral transition

Law-based reform has changed the role of headteachers. Emphasis moves on from pedagogy, to managerial practices, to politics, to community leadership, and to moral agency. Similar changes have been noticed in this study, in UK research (Davies and Ellison 1997; Earley *et al.* 2002), and in the US (Seashore-Louis and Murphy 1994; Talbot and Crow 1998). How are these changes connected to law-based reform? Three points emerge from this study: first, the school's infrastructure should adapt to the new demands from headteachers (Morrison 2002); second, schools should be able to adopt flexible structures and flexible targets (Bell 2003; Davies and Davies 2003a; Davies and Ellison 1997; Morrison 2002); and third, the moral role of headteaching and the need for ethical tools to reach moral judgements (Bottery 1992; Fullan 2003).

First, changing and adopting a new infrastructure is an important factor in headteachers' ability to cope with law-based reform that promotes decentralisation, standards, accountability, and quasi-market policies – in short, their ability to cope with instability and complexity (Morrison 2002). Obviously, operating in the ever-changing environment typical of law-based reform under Labour government, requires headteachers to develop new levels of alertness, sharpness, and planning, what is called 'strategic planning' in current literature (Bell 2003; Davies and Davies 2003a). Bell cautions that this idea is a bit of a myth, and very difficult to achieve in real daily life conditions in schools. Difficulties include headteachers becoming 'hero innovators' (Bell 2003: 94), the narrow scope of effectiveness measurement, and the labelling of schools as either 'good or bad'. Altogether, this is the lack of

> Any clear conceptual rationale that links the characteristics that commonly describe an effective school with a dynamic model of school processes in such a way that it might be possible to establish and explain the relationships between those characteristics and improved performance.... New Labour policy in this regard rests largely on exhortation and a battery of tactics, the precise outcome of which, are, at best, indeterminate.
>
> (Bell 2003: 96–7)

One of the shortcomings of law-based reform is that it creates immediate large-scale change, and assumes it occurs nearly at once, but of course it takes much longer. It turns deep, cultural change into technical arrangements (Harris 1999). Leadership and school culture are big ships that find it difficult to change course. The price headteachers and schools pay is dear: anxiety, pressures, and often – failure. Training and other scaffolding come later, if at all. However, what can be said in favour of law-based reform is that it might be the only way to create real change in an unaccountable system that is primarily conservative and a bit scared of change, and that was also judged, for a long period, on its continuity and stability, rather than its innovation. Building capacity of school staff to confront and compete, adapt and develop, is an extremely complex undertaking (Harris 2001; Stoll and Earl 2003). Many of the useful factors are inner school ones, and are dependent on the headteacher and his or her leadership qualities, in their widest sense. These include what has already been found in numerous studies (Chatwin 2003; Friedman 2003; Gold and Evans 2002; James 2003; Ogawa and Bossert 2000; Sergiovanni 1995; Stoll and Earl 2003): the adoption of transformational and collaborative leadership styles, which will not be discussed here. But law-based reform also has an important role in creating the appropriate conditions for evolving agents' capacity. According to Stoll and Earl, these include: a much greater respect on the part of authorities for professionalism and the professional opinions of those involved in education within schools; supporting professional development, financially and organisationally; understanding, truly and sincerely, that not all schools are the same; encouraging schools to organise networks; and, finally, to offer true 'critical friendship' (Stoll and Earl 2003: 502). The headteachers in this study report that some of these factors do exist. In some places, supervisors and LEA officials do offer critical friendships. There is an attempt to boost headteachers' professional knowledge by offering new types of training both for acting heads (LPSH) and aspiring heads (NPQH).[3] The establishment of the National Council for School Leaders is in itself an important statement. Government money for partnerships with universities, like the ones with the NCSL and the London Leadership Centre, are good examples. It seems, however, that there is not enough support for intensive high-standard academic training that offers philosophical,. sociological, methodological, and administrative foundations for headteachers. Such training can be found in Masters and doctoral programmes on educational management, administration, and leadership; as well as law-based requirements for school headteachers. Research shows that professions gained social, political, and public status when they became connected with academic institutions on a regular basis, including the development of new, specific, academic degrees with specific titles that are also a precondition for certification and application for a post (Gibton 2000; Milstein 1990; Murphy 1992; Whitaker 1997).

The second point is the ability of schools to explore new directions and tasks and adopt some 'businesslike' practices of opening new markets (Morrison 2002). For instance, Davies (1997) found that school resources are often used only partially and that buildings, ICT equipment, and even school staff can be utilised more efficiently and profitably. Hentchke and Davies (1997) offer a taxonomy of managerial decisions that headteachers in a changing environment need to consider for their schools, including:

1. Decisions about what business to be in.
2. Decisions about how to organise and operate the production process or service delivery of the organisation.
3. Decisions about the kinds of labour to employ and how that labour is compensated.
4. Decisions about the customers and clients to be served.

                                                   (Hentchke and Davies 1997: 28)

Such considerations are also valid for policy makers pursuing law-based reform, because encouraging headteachers to adopt these practices can help achieve law-based reform's goals much faster and more efficiently. Anthony's comprehensive presented in Chapter 3 is this kind of school. As the reader may remember, Anthony opened a 'mini college' that teaches English and ICT to Muslim Bengali women, using school facilities and offering some members of the staff extra work, pay, and professional interest. It is also Anthony's way of counteracting the government's initiative of taking away the school's sixth form. Law-based reform can help by creating frameworks for schools wishing to go into new types of business, and offer headteachers suitable training. Training programmes and performance-related pay (for teachers) are both mechanisms that encourage schools in this direction. Perhaps by some financial backing or matching, schools can be encouraged to pursue new avenues of education. As Stoll and Earl (2003) suggest, *schools are not the same*; it is the dissimilarities among them that allow some schools to pursue new initiatives, and, in this case, especially inner city schools situated among diverse communities (both socio-economically and culturally). Morrison, whose original work is on the influence of chaos theory on schools in the postmodern society, provides a vivid example:

> There is a teaching headteacher of a small four-teacher rural village primary ... which serves a remote introverted area where employment options for adults are either farming or nothing. The school enjoys good relationships with parents, but this does not extend beyond formal meetings and visits for 'special events'. The headteacher is disenchanted with recent government reforms of education, as ... they are removing him from those parts of his work for which he came into teaching – working with children, instructional leadership, professional autonomy, and informed pedagogical freedom, teaching and a set of values for a liberal arts and humanistic tradition of education.... He decides to take early retirement. The new headteacher decides that the children need to be equipped to take their place in new employment markets, probably outside the neighbourhood. She feels that the horizons of the local population need to be extended ... she discusses with the teachers ... and through a series of open meetings with the parents.... This leads to the establishment of a range of 'out of hours' classes in IT for adults, the school becomes a centre for job advertising and for Internet Links ... a small building programme takes place to convert rooms into a learner-resource suite, and parent-assistants come into the schools ... within one year the school has changed from a slightly sleepy, if well-intentioned and friendly place, into a vibrant community with links and connections to the outside.... The school has moved from benevolent autocracy to participatory democracy. Children and parents have raised aspirations.
>
> (Morrison 2002: 5–6)

The final point in this section is about ethics and the moral commitment of headteachers, which are especially important when schools are pushed towards a managerial culture of performativity (Ball 2003) and accountability. How can headteachers remain committed to values like equality and multiculturalism in a culture that might push them towards performance at all costs? Moral deliberation is therefore important. Moreover, among competing values, clients, and constituencies, it is important to locate those towards which the headteacher is more committed. Figure 6.3 presents a model for assessing this situation.

The model was based on concepts and research on the nature of professions (Koehn 1994; Schon 1983; Starr 1982). Professional codes of ethics provide the members of the profession, among other things, with clear definitions of fidelity. Such definitions are needed because professionals often face dilemmas that evolve around conflicts of fidelity and affinity to various groups of people, institutions, or values. All professionals are obliged to various audiences such as peers and colleagues, the law, the general public, and their paying clients. In the semi-professions or in human-services organisations, but also in a classic profession like medicine (when it is dispersed under the auspices of a public health service), the problem of delivering professional service in a bureaucratic state-financed system adds more conflict. The 'classic' professional sits in his or her private office waiting for a client to choose them on a mutual recognition of the client's need and the professional's reputation. The state-employed professional usually does not choose the client and sometimes vice versa as well, that is the student does not always choose the school, the teacher, or the 'treatment' he or she will receive. Bureaucratic institutions often control the professional discretion on how to 'treat' the client, monitoring budget, time, and other allocation of resources. Bureaucratic systems also tend to control the professional's loyalty. The model in Figure 6.3 differentiates between headteachers' obligation, or *affinity*, to their colleagues, to the school governing body, and to the state, and their *fidelity* to one population alone: their students – with some strong ties to the students' parents (as their legal guardians), and to the immediate community of the school. As discussed previously, headteachers

Figure 6.3 *Headteachers' fidelity and affinity: a possible model*

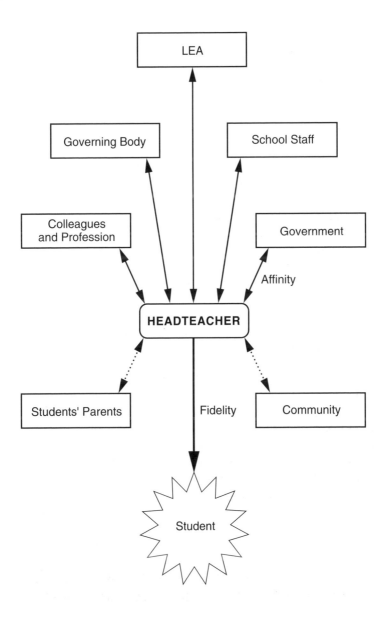

need a broad outlook on educational policy to succeed in the new system. This has a moral aspect as well. Michael Fullan (2003) who studies examples from the UK, from Canada, and from the US, writes about 'moral imperatives of school leadership'. He, too, thinks moral viewpoints are a basic requirement for headteachers in decentralised systems, and talks about factors that contribute to this within schools and on the system level:

> The overall environment must improve for all schools to continually improve. The environment cannot improve only from the top. The top can provide a vision, policy incentives, mechanisms for interaction, coordination, and monitoring, but, to realise this vision, there must be a lateral development – that is, people at one's own level giving and receiving help ... across schools. In this way, the moral imperative becomes a palpable, collective endeavour. If these developments play themselves out regionally ... it is far more likely leaders will be cognisant of their responsibility and contributions to closing the performance gap beyond their own bailiwick.
>
> (Fullan 2003: 47)

According to Fullan, the headteacher must have a strong commitment to other schools and communities, over and above his or her own:

> School leaders of the future must become increasingly aware of the bigger picture. What is the role of the public school in society? What are the key educational issues at the provincial ... and national level? I don't mean principals should add saving society to their job description, but I do mean that they should be acutely aware of how the public education system is faring and how it is contributing to societal development, both in its own right and in comparison with other ... countries. The more that principals identify with this bigger picture, the more the moral purpose will become a feature of the whole system, thus improving more public schools.
>
> (Fullan 2003: 49–50)

This last point is important for decentralising law-based reform. The devolutionary features of the system strengthen individualism among school leaders. The latter develop a sense of personal survival – of themselves and their schools – which is encouraged by managerial ethics that speak in the language of a competitive market (Ball 1987; Bottery 1992). This situation is not just common to England, as Boyd writes on US education:

> One can argue abut the extent to which it is the *welfare* state or the *capitalist* state that has created or exacerbated the social problems and 'culture wars' … the increasing diversity of our society … multicultural, multi-faith, with alarming inequalities and permeable borders penetrated by globalisation, by immigration (often illegal) and by international terrorism … the hegemony of white majority and even of the English language are no longer assured; 'minority majorities' are emerging … and demographic trends indicate that this is the wave of the future. Most of the population growth is occurring in poor, disadvantaged families … for whom English is a second language.
>
> (Boyd 2004: 11, emphases in the original)

However, in contrast to the business world, schools operate in an interdependent environment. The survival of a school is not only influenced by its ability to 'knock out' competitors. The price the competitors' clients might pay is dear, ethically and morally, and this will have a direct influence on the working and living conditions of the 'winning' school's students when they grow up. Isolation may seem appealing in the production stage, but when those students who miss out grow up and become angry, frustrated adult citizens, then the relatively successful graduates are affected too. Such a utilitarian explanation is overshadowed by moral arguments. Strike (2004), who writes on the inherent conflicts among capitalism, democracy, and liberalism, sheds light on the concept of subjective versus objective legitimacy in public education.

> For an institution to be subjectively legitimate, it must be seen as legitimate. To be seen as legitimate, an institution must satisfy such criteria of legitimacy as are held by those it must please. There is no guarantee that these criteria will be reasonable. Schools may be expected to educate well and be just and democratic, but they may also be expected to

have winning football teams or to hire from a favoured ethnic group.
Yet it is subjective legitimacy that counts politically.

(Strike 2004: 27–38)

Strike cautions that efficiency is now seen as a major component of
legitimacy:

> While efficiency counts, it is not sufficient and the preoccupation with
> it can be unfortunate. Useful examples are the familiar debates about
> choice or decentralisation. These policies include proposals to change
> the governance of schools. They redistribute powers among parents,
> legislatures, and educators. They influence intellectual liberty and
> religious freedom ... such changes represent a shift in how core consti-
> tutional values are applied to schools.
>
> (Strike 2004: 38)

Strike thinks that schools not only have a duty to supply the demands of
subjective legitimacy, but also have to educate the public on objective
legitimacy as it occurs in a democratic, liberal society. Schools therefore
serve as institutions that are burdened with shaping society, and not just
supplying it with a service. Henry Giroux (1992), one of the leading
political and educational philosophers in the US, thinks schools should
be an arena of debate over values, rather than carriers of values that have
been accepted by power groups:

> Democracy is not simply a lifeless tradition or disciplinary subject....
> Neither ... an empty set of regulations and procedures that can be sub-
> sumed in the language of proficiency, efficiency, and accountability.
> Nor is it an outmoded moral and political referent that makes govern-
> ing more difficult in light of the rise of new rights and entitlements
> demanded by emerging social movements and groups. Put simply,
> democracy is both a discourse and a practice that produces particular
> narratives and identities informed by the principles of freedom, equality,
> and social justice. It is expressed not in moral platitudes but in concrete
> struggles and practices that find expression in classroom social relations
> ... the challenge of democracy resides in the recognition that educators,
> parents, and others must work hard to ensure that future generations

will view the idea and practice of democracy as a goal worth believing in and struggling for.

(Giroux 1992: 5)

Headteachers should, therefore, focus on students and clients but keep a watchful eye open for how their individual practices in one school, and one community, influence society, and promote certain values and powers within the democratic state. The headteachers in this study do, in fact, keep this eye open. Law-based reform should keep in mind that this is part of what good leadership is, and create appropriate conditions for it, and provide a much clearer direction than it does now. It must also separate between tools, including free market and accountability, economic and other efficiency measures, and the values these tools can serve, protect, and promote. When research (Brighouse *et al.* 2002; Gillborn and Youdell 2000) cautions that these tools do not necessarily achieve equality, and when headteachers such as those who took part in this study, both in strong areas and in weak areas, combine these findings with their own local field-oriented point of view, then the government should do some rethinking. One source of knowledge for law-based reform is the extensive research done in the US under the title of 'Urban Systemic Programs' (USP) (Calhoun 2002; Cibulka 1999; Davis and Gold 2002; Slavin 1999a, b; Thornton and Wongbundhit 2002; Vogel *et al.* 2002; Wong 1999). This is a set of initiatives, policies, and mandates that are implemented in large and problematic counties in the US's education system. These counties are characterised by having large numbers of schools (sometimes several hundred large secondary schools), large poor minority populations, and deteriorated urban areas. The conclusions from these studies are: only long-range proven programmes should be accepted; should be government controlled, as opposed to close liaisons between the government and the field or passing over control to private companies; an emphasis on local contexts, and close partnerships with local leaders, headteachers, parents, and school staff – despite the size of the projects – should be promoted; a keen national and political base, and support for change should be passed down; and finally, effort should be made to invest in research to establish a strong base of support for policy and accountability mechanisms, including study of the non-performative factors of reform, such as those mentioned in this chapter and book.

Towards the 'Educational Leadership Act' and the 'Education System Charter'

What seems to be missing from the mosaic of English law-based reforms, a welcome, and perhaps necessary addition to existing legislation, is what I shall term the 'Educational Leadership Act' and the 'Education System Charter'. The two laws are, of course, fictitious, but they could help a great deal in improving compatibility among headteachers, educational leadership, and law-based reform. The first law, on educational leadership, should deal with the following issues:

1. Defining the role of the headteacher as the CEO of the school.
2. Stating the utmost importance of educational leadership in managing English schools.
3. Establishing in primary law a set of responsibilities of headteachers.
4. Establishing in primary legislation the authority, jurisdiction, powers, and prerogatives of headteachers.
5. Determining some fundamentals of the basic infrastructure of self-managed schools, especially the duties, responsibilities, and even the mere existence of senior and middle management teams and their salaries.
6. Defining, differentiating, and stating the various affinities and obligations of headteachers and their duty towards students, towards the students' parents, and towards the community.
7. Defining government requirements regarding headteachers' training, education, and background.

The second law, on the education system, should deal with the following issues:

1. Provision of a clear structure of England's education system, including the place and role of the political tiers, including the DfES, the LEA, and other local or national providers (such as denominations), and the role of schools, including types and finance, and communities.
2. Provision of a clear mechanism of responsibility and authority, i.e. accountability in all of the above.

7 Conclusion: shortening the distance between law-based reform and educational leadership

Among worldwide attempts to introduce law-based reform, the English attempt probably has been one of the most comprehensive and consistent over the years. It is also the most centralised, for a relatively large country. Paradoxically, it is also one of the most decentralising law-based reforms. What made it so interesting to study is the transformation towards two-level legislation – the first, which introduced free market policy under the Conservative government, and the second, which attempted to retake control under Labour. This attempt, to influence the free market policy and implement a 'third way' ideology, makes the claim that law-based reform should address educational leadership, a legitimate claim. The field of law-based reform is not separate from the field of educational leadership. Conceptually, they are distinct. Practically, they are linked and interdependent. Law-based reform has profound influence on the shaping of educational administration and leadership. The redefinition of the components and responsibilities of the system has immanent influence on the role, the job description, and the qualities of leadership. Educational leadership, in its turn, has an important impact on the possibilities and prospects of law-based reform to attain its goals. Educational leaders have a pivotal role in the realisation of law-based reform – as long as they understand it, believe in it, and identify with it. If, however, headteachers do not support it, then its chances of success will be limited. Law-based reform has to address educational leadership. It cannot, as unfortunately has been done in several countries and not just in England, regard head-teachers as a natural by-product of reform.

The hidden agenda of school reform is currently twofold and contra-dictory. On the one hand, headteachers are perceived as omnipotent, great leaders, flexible enough to incorporate and implement huge cultural and organisational changes swiftly and effectively. On the other hand, simultaneously, the very same headteachers are perceived as conservative, frightened individuals, who delay and obstruct the course of change and reform. Addressing educational leaders in law-based reform should balance these two dichotomous images and offer a more balanced and less conflictual solution or approach. The current situation is that educational leaders – headteachers – are left behind by law-based reform, which in turn seriously threatens law-based reform's chances of reaching its targets. Leadership and headship should be treated systematically, as are other pivotal components of the system, such as LEAs and governing bodies.

The English case of law-based reform has some local characteristics, but many parts of the story presented in this book are quite global, or at least relevant to other democracies that have the Anglo-American ethos of education as an emancipatory and empowering mechanism. All over the world, law-based reform is becoming a widespread serious alternative for other educational policy tools. From Tennessee, via Alberta, to England – with many more stops on the way – there is a ruling paradigm. This is the paradigm of linear sanctity. As law-based reform carries with it a hidden presupposition that: (1) policy is indeed linear; and (2) by designing the macro-components of the system, the micro-politics of the school, including the important issue of educational leadership, administration, and management, can be designed. This proposition is more of an axiom, a dream, not an empirical fact. A link or correlation does exist, but this correlation is intricate and mysterious. Improving the understanding of this link and shedding some light on how it emerges was one of the targets of the study presented in this book. But further and deeper understanding needs much more work. Law-based reform often treats people as computers. This metaphor is not unique to the English system, but it becomes more evident when law is used frequently. While computers treat all input at the same level of importance, regardless of when it was saved, people tend to address the new more seriously than the old. When reforms pile up quickly, one on top of the other, without sufficient time for the fundamentals of reform to sink in, the reforms lose their dramatic effect.

Headteachers in this study started off with great respect, and basic curiosity towards the law. This attitude is waning, and is being replaced by a shrewd sense of politics and survival tactics. Government should take heed of this as a warning sign. The 2002 ongoing legislation (EA 2002) and strategy papers (DfES 2002) suggest that this lesson has not been internalised so far.

Strengthening educational leaders and equipping them with sufficient capacity tools can balance problematic forces of subjective legitimacy (Strike 2004) and the perils of takeover forces that are not delicate enough, as well as the advantages that some groups have in a market situation due to cultural capital (Boyd 2004; Hannaway 2004). The headteachers' proximity to pedagogical situations can correct the flaws and defects that are the natural by-product of large-scale law-based reform.

Finally, government should make equality its primary concern, not only because of its importance, not only because of evident socio-economic gaps, but because other major concerns of the system can be controlled and promoted through decentralisation and quasi-markets. Equality is the one issue that needs constant and unrelenting government support or it will not happen.

With respect to research, it is already clear that the existing paradigms are not sufficient for the complex layouts required for understanding educational policy. The growing rifts between the naturalistic and positivist paradigms and between the distinct fields of educational policy and of educational administration and leadership, are not helpful. This study can, at best, along with others, be a catalyst to the debate on this issue. What is required is a new paradigm of educational research in educational policy. This paradigm should mould together conceptual frameworks from the fields of educational law, educational policy, educational administration, and educational leadership. This paradigm should manufacture a fusion of methodologies that will engulf the advantages of positivist and naturalist paradigms, of quantitative and qualitative methods, of a large-scale representative sampling process, coupled with small-scale, but in-depth, case studies. As educational reality becomes much more complex and dynamic than it was before, the tools to explore, describe, and understand this reality have to be multi-paradigmatic, multi-method and multi-conceptual as well.

It is important to point out that the principals who took part in this study make a distinct separation between the *policies* that are established under the law and the fact that *law is indeed the tool by which policy is established*. Throughout this study, I asked myself how these two variables – the use of law as a policy tool and the policy itself – become entwined and whether they can be separated at all. This study does not give a complete answer to this problem but it should give a partial one. The fact that educational law goes into so many details regarding schools, curricula, human resource management, retention, attainment, etc., gives English headteachers a sense that the government and the general public suddenly see education as a central and dynamic issue, after decades of its being somewhat dull and unchanging.

Support mechanisms are necessary for those schools and headteachers which are marginalised by law-based reform. Such mechanisms should include management training and setting up legal and financial aid groups that can serve several schools in budget planning, legal advice, and such. In rural areas, some of this help may be web-based for greater effectiveness and lower cost.

The story of headteachers under the Labour government since 1997 is a vibrant, vigorous tale of educational leadership on the school level but also on the national level – for what is law-based reform if not exercise of leadership? Law-based reform offers new horizons, prospects, and changes for educational leadership. Headship has become exciting. However, pressures are building up, and it is up to law-based reform, policy makers, and lawmakers to take responsibility on leadership capacities. This will not only improve leadership but also allow law-based reform to achieve its aims. This is not a story of irresponsible reform. The Labour government's law-based reform is a bold and important attempt to create a truly 'third way'. Mistakes have been made but turning headteachers into allies can really assist lawmakers. Attentive, unbiased, honourable listening to headteachers is a good start. Recognising partnerships with them and empowering them formally and legally, can be the next step.

Appendix: conceptual framework and method of the study

This is a qualitative multiple case study (Stake 1997) that utilised the naturalistic paradigm (Denzin and Lincoln 2000; Lincoln and Guba 2000; Lincoln and Denzin 2000; Maykut and Morehouse 1994; Vidich and Lyman 2000) and tools combined with a quantitative-type sampling process (Gibton 2004).

The method and layout of this study narrates the headteachers' and stakeholders' 'landscapes' (Connelly and Clandinin 1996) and 'mindscapes' (Sergiovanni 1995) concerning system decentralisation, system and school restructuring, educational leadership, and school-based management. According to Sergiovanni, mindscapes are like road maps, that 'provide rules, images and principles that define what the principalship is and how its practice should unfold' (Sergiovanni 1995: 30). Connelly and Clandinin use a related term: 'working landscape'. Although this term relates to research on teachers' knowledge, it is useful for studying the implications of policy among headteachers and stakeholders too. 'Landscapes' are used to disclose teacher's 'secret, sacred and cover stories (that) provided a map useful for studying the dynamics of the relations between teacher's personal practical and professional knowledge' (Connelly and Clandinin 1996: 25).

Understanding how policy is seen through the eyes of some of the main players in the field can add insights as to how policy is implemented and why it succeeds or fails (Bowman and Haggerson 1992). According to Bowman and Haggerson, interpretative inquiry can assist in connecting between 'informing policy' and 'informing practice'. While the first focuses 'on rules, written and unwritten, by which the educational institutions run, and on the problems that result from those rules', the latter is about 'the practitioner doing his or her practice' (Bowman and Haggerson

1992: 8). They use the metaphor of the researcher as a person sailing down a stream in a boat. His or her wish is to describe the stream, understand how it functions, and where it goes. The need to sail down the stream arises because 'there are some things about the stream that one cannot find by sitting on the edge' (Bowman and Haggerson 1992: 11). Now during his or her trip down the stream, the researcher may get wet and the boat may rock. The smells and sights remind the researcher of his or her personal experiences. Such a researcher is a participant observer. He or she is able to collect unique insights, valuable and essential for understanding the mechanism and effects of policy implementation. The researcher, who, according to Bowman and Haggerson, wishes to share his or her experience with others, has to 'report in such a way that the reader envisions being in the boat in the stream' (Bowman and Haggerson: 1992: 12). This metaphor is applicable to qualitative research in general and especially to its hermeneutic branches. But when policy is concerned, the role of the researcher is to identify the socio-political forces that are behind that policy 'through critical analysis ... emancipate themselves and others from them' (Bowman and Haggerson 1992: 14).

This is a process of demystification that relates to Sergiovanni's term 'mindscapes'. Mindscapes are the images that practitioners hold on the link among theory, research, and practice. According to Sergiovanni, there are three types of 'mindscapes' – 'mystics', 'neats', and 'scruffies' – shared by players in the field (e.g. headteachers) and researchers alike. 'Mystics' view educational administration as a tacit and intuitive occupation. 'Neats' see it as linked in a linear form to theory. To 'scruffies': 'educational administration resembles a craftlike science within which practice is characterised by interacting reflection and action episodes. Theory and research are only one source of knowledge ... designed to inform but not to prescribe practice' (Sergiovanni 1995: 30). The 'scruffy' point of view is useful when dealing with 'complex problems, that exist in turbulent environments under indeterminate conditions' (Sergiovanni 1995: 33), such as decentralisation policy in education. The disclosure of these 'landscapes' and 'mindscapes' is achieved by using in-depth qualitative (ethnographic) interviews and analysing authentic documents.

Sampling

The main part of the study included qualitative data that were gathered from 29 schools in southeast England, as shown in Table A.1. The sample included headteachers from six types of schools: grammar schools (elitist government financed and owned), LEA schools (also now known as community schools), foundation schools (formerly grant-maintained), religious schools (known as 'schools of faith', mainly CE – Church of England, and RC – Roman Catholic), specialist schools (including City Technology Colleges and 16–19 colleges), and EAZ schools (Education Action Zones). These types of school represent England's school system and main trends in educational policy from the 1990s (Gibton and Goldring 2002; Whitty *et al.* 1998).

Another body of data was gathered by sending a semi-structured tool to 200 headteachers in England, distributed according to the same principles applied to the first sample. Although response rate in this group was quite low (only 15 per cent) it provided useful information that supplemented the main data.

Table A.1 *Distribution of school sample according to school type and SES*

School type	Student population			
	Low-SES	Middle class	High-SES	Total
Grammar	–	2	2	**4**
LEA/Community	2	3	1	**6**
GM/Foundation	2	2	2	**6**
Faith (religious)	3		1	**4**
Specialised		2	2	**4**
EAZ	5			**5**
Total	**12**	**9**	**8**	**29**

Note: n = 29.

Research tools

Research tools included in-depth interviews with headteachers (primary tool), collected written material from within the schools (such as school prospectuses, OFSTED reports, etc.), and some participant observations. The interviews with the headteachers lasted between 1.5 and 3 hours. A typical interview began with an open question that directed the interviewees to talk about their job in general. The questions that followed emerged from the interview itself (Fontana and Frey 2000; Maykut and Morehouse 1994; Patton 1980). 'Could you give me an example?', 'Please talk more about this', and 'What do you mean?' were typical questions (see detailed interview plan at the end of the Appendix). The final part of the interview included presentation findings from other schools or from research, but this was only done when the authentic part of the interview was over. Visits to the 29 schools included some open observation before and after the interviews, to obtain a general impression of the school. All schools were photographed, including their neighbourhoods.

The second sample was studied by sending an open-ended questionnaire to the headteachers, to be returned by mail:

- Please name three areas of your work where educational law has the MOST influence.
- In what way does educational law influence your work?
- Do you feel that educational law is accompanied by the necessary means, tools, and resources for advancing and implementing your school's aims? Which are provided and which are missing?

Data analysis

Data analysis was aimed at coding and categorising the headteachers' stories and forming some graphic maps. The maps attempt to show the main players in the fields of educational policy as well as legal issues (divided into legislation, litigation, and administrative directives) that exist in educational policy in England, according to the headteachers.

These findings were analysed and presented in graphic charts. Content analysis included coding, building, and defining distinct categories as is common to grounded theory constant comparative methods (Charmaz 2000; Hutchinson 1988; Strauss 1987; Strauss and Corbin 1994). The stories of the headteachers and their schools were analysed in three con-secutive levels. First, all data were categorised into small sections, or statements, typically one or several sentences long. Second, the unit of analysis was an 'episode', typically a few paragraphs long, in which the headteacher presented a detailed example or told a short story. These stories emphasise the headteachers' roles as 'tribe elders' and as carriers of school culture (Sergiovanni 1995). Third, whole school and headteacher stories were analysed. All along this process, two types of categories were defined. *Emic* categories were constructed by identifying repetitions and phrasing their characteristics and criteria, from the raw data. *Etic* categories were constructed by using several models from literature on educational administration, policy, and leadership (Vidich and Lyman 2000). These included, for instance, Ogawa *et al.*'s (1999) model on school dilemmas, Adams and Kirst's (1999) model on educational account-ability and leadership, and Glatter's (2002, 2003) models of governance. While analysing the stories, several 'independent' variables such as types of schools, students' SES and area were considered as well. The analysis in both stages of the study included disclosure of the headteachers' 'mindscapes' (Sergiovanni 1995) and 'landscapes' (Connelly and Clandinin 1996) concerning the English educational system and their schools' place-ment within it, as well as their concepts of educational law and its role in educational policy and decentralisation reform efforts. This was done by building a hierarchy of categories including the spotting and formulating of 'core categories' (Strauss 1987), and finally forming graphic maps from these categories.

Validity

Finally, the maps that emerged from the analysis were validated with a group of headteachers from the sample, and further corrected and readjusted. Specific maps were then constructed to differentiate between types of headteachers, types of schools, etc.

Ethics

All headteachers gave informed consent and were promised complete anonymity.

UK study – Head Interview Plan

Interview
General title: please talk about your work and the law. How is your work influenced by law. You can talk on 'larger' policy issues (e.g. decentralisation, national curriculum, funding, enrolment/expulsion) and 'smaller ones (e.g. health and safety).

Authentic part/Emic questions
(Patton, 1990; Maykut and Morehouse, 1994)
(all questions can be asked in past, present, future)
- Who was with you?
- What was it like being there?
- What did you do then?
- How are you going to deal with this?
- Tell me more about this?
- Can you give me an example?
- I'm not sure I understand – can you explain this to me?
- This is very helpful, can you elaborate on that?
- What do you think of this?
- Is this good or bad?
- How did you feel when that happened?
- What do you know about this?
- Who took part/worked with you on this?

Structured part/Etic questions (After two-thirds of interview)
- Quote other heads – receive reaction/response.
- Ask how your leadership/accountability are affected by law.
- Ask whether adequate capacity tools are provided.
- Ask who is the owner/constituency of the head.
- Ask for senior/middle management team members. Who nominates them.
- Ask for relationship with DfEE/governors/LEA/LEA supervisor.
- Ask about Ofsted inspection/PANDAS/league tables.
- Ask how equitable education is affected by these new policies.

Ask: for other principals to interview (what school, name and phone no.)!
Thanks!

Notes

Introduction

1 Throughout this book I use the term 'headteacher' which is common in England; the US equivalent is 'principal'. These are perhaps not just semantic differences: they touch the core and essence of the idea of educational leadership and its personification in schools. These differences will be explored further in this book.

1 Law-based reform

1 Office for Standards in Education; National Assessment of Educational Progress; Council of Ministers of Education of Canada/School Achievement Indicators Program.

2 'Primary legislation' is a legal term, part of what is known as the 'pyramid of norms' which is part of every legal system. This means that norms in every such system are derived from higher norms, and at the top is the basic or ground norm, usually in the form of a written or (as is the case in England) an unwritten constitution. Next in line is primary legislation, e.g. laws passed in parliament. Then comes secondary legislation, which includes regulations, and then administrative directives, circulars, and so on.

3 This is a UK legal term for a final bill presented to Parliament, and becomes primary legislation. Before the White Paper, a 'Green Paper' is circulated allowing public debate on the proposed bill.

4 The US term resegregation is problematic in this context, for England's school system was never really integrated, certainly not purposely. There was no bussing mechanism between high and low SES areas, or between minority, refugee, and middle-class predominately white

areas. However, the comprehensive high school was probably more inclusive than other types of schools that flourished under New Labour from the late 1990s.

2 The leadership agenda of English law-based reform

1   Education (School Teacher Appraisal) (England) Regulations 2001.
2   In the United States, law-based reform is both state and federal. Most of the legislation is indeed in the state level. State legislature is 'American' for state parliament.

3 Strong laws – strong schools

1   Headteachers' statements are presented in their own words, with only the occasional very minor amendments for clarification. I have maintained the accuracy of the quotes to keep the authenticity of the comments and to convey a sense of the headteachers' feelings.
2   In order to preserve the privacy of the schools studied throughout the cases presented in this book, the headteachers' names and basic data on the headteachers and the schools, have been changed to avoid any possibility of recognition. The complete stories and details are kept safe with the author.

5 English law-based reform in the eyes of headteachers

1   This was determined by the number of statements on each issue and the volume of each statement (Miles and Huberman 1991). The phrasing and clustering of issues is also the result of data analysis.
2   As these lines are written, the following news item was published on Sky website:

Snap school inspections
A major shake-up in the way schools are inspected, involving more frequent checks and less warning for teachers is being announced. OFSTED says giving as little as one day's notice will enable it to assess

accurately how a school operates. But union leaders say the approach risks rough justice for headteachers. The plans include halving the gap between inspections from six to three years for most schools and slashing advance warning from up to 10 weeks to as little as a single working day. Chief inspector David Bell said the changes would enable OFSTED to 'present a warts and all picture of schools as we find them, not how schools wish to be found'.

'Shorter, sharper'

He launched a two-month consultation on his proposals, which will require changes to the law governing OFSTED. If ministers agree to find time in the next parliamentary session, the so-called 'shorter, sharper' inspections could begin in autumn 2005, Mr Bell said.

School standards minister David Miliband said: 'The current inspection process has played an important role in the drive to raise standards but it is right to seek improvements that will deliver a sharper focus, lighter touch and clearer link to school improvement in the future.'

David Hart, general secretary of the National Association of Head Teachers, said: 'NAHT supports the chief inspector's plans to cut the bureaucracy, red tape and the ever-increasing cost of the OFSTED regime.

Standards

'But if he doesn't deal with the fundamental concerns regarding the new framework, and in particular the ever-increasing demand for higher standards and the poor quality of some of the inspection teams, then heads and teachers will say that this is only a job half done.'

John Bangs, head of education at the National Association of Schoolmasters Union of Women Teachers, said: 'What I'm concerned about is the combination of two working days' notice and shorter, sharper inspections.

'I think there's a real danger of rough justice in these proposals.

'Of course we need to reduce the amount of anxiety time but he needs to look at what appears to be a developing campaign to use inspections to lever up standards, instead of to help teachers in the classroom.'

(SKY news website, 10 February 2004
http://www.sky.com/skynews/home)

3 *Studies in Educational Evaluation* (SEE).
4 See for instance:
http://www.telegraph.co.uk/education/main.jhtml
http://education.guardian.co.uk/
5 See also: SI 630 Education (School Information) Regulations 1981, and SI 1502 Education (School Information) (England) Regulations 1993.

6 English law-based reform

1 Of course, schools in Britain were never segregated *stricto sensu* as they were in the US in the pre-Brown era (1954), so 'integration' is the appropriate term when dealing with UK schools.
2 The term 'public schools' has been attributed in England to private, elitist schools. However, in this chapter and in fact in this whole book, the term is used as a synonym for what is called in England 'maintained' schools, and in the United States 'public' schools or 'public education'.
3 See: SI 3111 Education (Head Teachers' Qualifications) (England) Regulations 2003.

Bibliography

Statutes and statutory instruments

Education Reform Act 1988, ISBN 0 10 544088 4
Education Act 1993, ISBN 0 10 543593 7
Education Act 1996, ISBN 0 10 545696 9
School Inspections Act 1996, ISBN 0 10 545796 5
School Standards and Framework Act 1998, ISBN 0 10 543198 2
Education Act 2002, ISBN 0 10 543202 4
Education (School Teacher Appraisal) (England Regulations 2001)
School Governance (Constitution) (England) Regulations 2003
Statutory Instrument No. 543 The Education (Teachers) Regulations 1993
Statutory Instrument No. 3111 Education (Head Teachers' Qualifications) (England)
  Regulations 2003

Books, articles, and papers

Ackerman, R.H. and Maslin-Ostrowski, P. (2002) *The Wounded Leader: How Real Leadership Emerges in Times of Crisis.* San Francisco: Jossey-Bass.

Adams, J.E. and Kirst, M.W. (1999) New demands for educational accountability: striving for results in an era of excellence. In Murphy, J. and Seashore-Louis, K. (eds), *Handbook of Research on Educational Administration* (pp. 463–89). San Francisco: Jossey-Bass.

Apple, M. (1995) *Education and Power* (2nd edn). New York: Routledge.

Arthur, J. (1998) British human rights legislation and religiously affiliated schools and colleges. *Education and the Law*, 10 (4): 225.

Aspin, D.N. and Chapman, J.D. (1994) *Quality Schooling: A Pragmatic Approach to Some Current Problems, Topics and Issues.* New York: Cassell.

Ball, S. (1987) *The Micro-politics of the School: Towards a Theory of School Organization.* London: Routledge.

—— (1994) What is policy? Texts, trajectories and toolboxes. In Ball, S. (ed.), *Education Reform: A Critical and Post-Structural Approach* (pp. 15–27). Buckingham: Open University Press.

—— (2003) The teacher's soul and the terrors of performativity. *Journal of Educational Policy*, 18 (2): 215–28.

Barth, R.S. (1986) The principalship. *Educational Leadership*, 42 (6): 92–104.

Beaudin, B.Q., Thompson, J.S., and Jacobson, L. (2002) The administrator paradox: more certified, fewer apply. Paper presented at the annual meeting of the American Educational Research Association, New Orleans, April.

Bell, L. (2003) Strategic planning in schools: a critical perspective. In Davies B. and West-Burnham, J. (eds), *Handbook of Educational Leadership and Management* (pp. 93–9). London: Pearson.

Bell, L. and Bush, T. (2002) The policy context. In Bush, T. and Bell, L. (eds), *The Principles and Practice of Educational Management* (pp. 3–14). London: Paul Chapman/Sage.

Bennett, N., Glatter, R., and Levacic, R. (eds) (1994) *Improving Educational Management through Research and Consultancy*. Open University Press/Paul Chapman/Sage.

Biddle, B.J. and Anderson, D.S. (1990) Social Research and Educational Change. In Anderson, D.S. and Biddle, B.J. (eds), *Knowledge for Policy: Improving Education through Policy* (pp. 1–20). London: Falmer Press.

Booth, P. and Bussell, H. (1999) Parental choice of primary schools: the legal implications and parental perceptions. *Education and the Law*, 11 (4): 295–308.

Bottery, M. (1992) *The Ethics of Educational Management: Personal, Social and Political Perspectives on School Organization*. London: Cassell.

—— (2000) *Education, Policy, and Ethics*. London: Continuum.

—— (2003) Globalization and the educational policy context. In Davies B. and West-Burnham, J. (eds), *Handbook of Educational Leadership and Management* (pp. 155–64). London: Pearson.

Bowman, A.C. and Haggerson, N.L. (1992) *Informing Educational Policy and Practice through Interpretive Inquiry*. Lancaster, PA: Technomic.

Boyd, W.L. (1988) Policy analysis, educational policy, and management: through a glass darkly? In Boyan, N. (ed.), *Handbook of Research on Educational Administration* (pp. 501–22). New York: Longman.

—— (2004) Public education's crisis of performance and legitimacy: rationale and overview of the yearbook. In Boyd, W.L. and Miretzky, D. (eds), *American Educational Governance on Trial: Change and Challenges – the 102nd Yearbook of the National Society for the Study of Education (NSSE)* (pp. 1–19). Chicago: Chicago University Press.

Bradney, A. (1996) Christian worship? *Education and the Law*, 8 (2): 127.

Brighouse, T., Howell, T., and Water, M. (2002) The learning city: before, during, after. Paper presented at the annual conference of the British Educational

Leadership, Management, and Administration Society (BELMAS), Birmingham, UK, September.

Brown, A. (1986) *Modern Political Philosophy: Theories of the Just Society*. London: Penguin Books.

Brown, D.J. (1990) *Decentralization and School-Based Management*. London: Falmer Press.

Bush, T., Coleman, M., and Glover, D. (1993) *Managing Autonomous Schools: The Grant Maintained Experience*. London: Paul Chapman.

Caldwell, B.J. (1993) The changing role of the school principal. In Dimmock, C. (ed.), *School-Based Management and Effectiveness* (pp. 165–84). London: Routledge.

—— (2000) Local management and learning outcomes: mapping the links in three generations of international research. In Coleman, M. and Anderson, L. (eds), *Managing Finance and Resources in Education* (pp. 24–40). London: Paul Chapman/Sage.

—— (2002) Autonomy and self-management: concepts and evidence. In Bush, T. and Bell, L. (eds), *The Principles and Practice of Educational Management* (pp. 34–48). London: Paul Chapman/Sage.

Calhoun, D. (2002) Evaluating a systemic reform project at the school district level. Paper presented at the annual meeting of the American Educational Research Association, New Orleans, April.

Charmaz, K. (2000) Grounded theory: objectivist and constructivist methods. In Denzin, N.K. and Lincoln, Y.S. (eds), *Handbook of Qualitative Research* (2nd edn) (pp. 509–36). Thousand Oaks, CA: Sage.

Chatwin, R. (2003) Subject leaders and their new headteachers: a study of strategic change in six English secondary schools. Paper presented at the annual conference of the British Educational Leadership, Management, and Administration Society (BELMAS), Kent Hill, UK, October.

Cheng, Y.C. (2000) The characteristics of Hong Kong school principals' leadership: the influence of societal culture. *Asia-Pacific Journal of Education*, 20 (2): 68–86.

Chubb, J.E. and Moe, T.M. (1990) *Politics, Markets and America's Schools*. Washington, DC: Brookings.

Cibulka, J.G. (1999) Moving toward an accountable system of K-12 education: alternative approaches and challenges. In Cizek, G.J. (ed.), *Handbook of Educational Policy* (pp. 184–213). San Diego: Academic Press.

—— (2004) Educational bankruptcy, takeovers, and reconstitution. In Boyd, W.L. and Miretzky, D. (eds), *American Educational Governance on Trial: Change and Challenges – the 102nd Yearbook of the National Society for the Study of Education (NSSE)* (pp. 271–90). Chicago: Chicago University Press.

—— and Derlin, R.L. (1998) Authentic education accountability policies: implementation of state initiatives in Colorado and Maryland. In Macpherson, R.J.S. (ed.), *The Politics of Accountability: Educative and International Perspectives* (pp. 79–92). Thousand Oaks, CA: Corwin Press.

Cizek, G.J. and Ramaswamy, V. (1999) American educational policy: constructing crises and crafting solutions. In Cizek, G.J. (ed.), *Handbook of Educational Policy* (pp. 498–522). San Diego: Academic Press.

Clark-Lindle, J. (2002) Validating the obvious: trauma and stress in the principal's office. Paper presented at the annual meeting of the American Educational Research Association, New Orleans, April.

Conley, D.T. (1997) *Roadmap to Restructuring: Charting the Course of Change in American Education.* Eugene, OR: ERIC.

—— and Goldman, P. (1994) Ten propositions for facilitative leadership. In Murphy, J. and Seashore-Louis, K. (eds), *Reshaping the Principalship: Insights from Transformational Reform Efforts* (pp. 237–64). Thousand Oaks, CA: Corwin Press.

Connelly, M.F. and Clandinin, J.D. (1996) Teachers' professional knowledge landscapes: teacher stories – stories of teachers – school stories – stories of schools. *Educational Researcher*, 25 (3): 24–30.

Davies, B. (1997) Rethinking the educational context: a reengineering approach. In Davies, B. and Ellison, L. (eds), *School Leadership for the 21st Century: A Competency and Knowledge Approach* (pp. 11–22). London: Routledge.

—— (2003) Reengineering: rethinking the school as an organisation. In Davies, B. and West-Burnham, J. (eds), *Handbook of Educational Leadership and Management* (pp. 100–6). London: Pearson.

—— and Davies, B. (2003a) Strategy and planning in schools. In Davies, B. and West-Burnham, J. (eds), *Handbook of Educational Leadership and Management* (pp. 79–92). London: Pearson.

—— and —— (2003b) Marketing schools: an analysis for educational leaders. In Davies, B. and West-Burnham, J. (eds), *Handbook of Educational Leadership and Management* (pp. 121–9). London: Pearson.

—— and Ellison, L. (1997) *School Leadership for the 21st Century: A Competency and Knowledge Approach.* London: Routledge.

Davis, D. and Gold, N. (2002) Urban systemic reforms: a discussion among policy makers, implementors, and evaluators interactive symposium: cross site evaluation of the urban systemic program. Paper presented at the annual meeting of the American Educational Research Association, New Orleans, April.

Dellar, G.B. (1994) Implementing school decision-making groups: a case study in restructuring. Paper presented at the annual meeting of the American Research Association, New Orleans, April.

DeMitchell, T.A. and Fossey, R. (1997a) *The Limits of Law-Based School Reform.* Lancaster, PA: Technomic.

—— and —— (1997b) Improving our children's future: looking beyond law-based school reform. In DeMitchell, T.A. and Fossey, R. (eds), *The Limits of Law-Based School Reform* (pp. 183–93). Lancaster, PA: Technomic.

Denzin, N.K. and Lincoln, Y.S. (2000) Introduction: the discipline and practice of qualitative research. In Denzin, N.K. and Lincoln, Y.S. (eds), *Handbook of Qualitative Research* (2nd edn) (pp. 1–29). Thousand Oaks, CA: Sage.

DfEE (1998) *Education Action Zone Handbook* (www.open.gov.uk/dfee/education/index.htm)

DfES (2002) *Education and Skills: Delivering Results A Strategy to 2006* (revised edn: December 2002).

Dimmock, C. (1993) School-based management and linkage with the curriculum. In Dimmock, C. (ed.), *School-Based Management and Effectiveness* (pp. 1–21). London: Routledge.

Earley, P. (2000) Monitoring, managing or meddling? Governing bodies and the evaluation of school performance. *Educational Management and Administration*, 28 (2): 199–210.

—— and Creese, M. (2003) Lay or professional? Re-examining the role of school governors in England. In Davies, B. and West-Burnham, J. (eds), *Handbook of Educational Leadership and Management* (pp. 246–55). London: Pearson.

—— Evans, J., Collarbone, P., Gold, A., and Halpin, D. (2002) *Establishing the Current State of School Leadership in England.* Norwich/London: Institute of Education, University of London/DfES.

Elmore, R.F. (1993) School decentralization: who gains? Who loses? In Hannaway, J. and Carnoy, M. (eds), *Decentralization and School Improvement* (pp. 33–46). San Francisco: Jossey-Bass.

Finn, C.E. (1990) What ails education research? In Anderson, D.S. and Biddle, B.J. (eds), *Knowledge for Policy: Improving Education through Policy* (pp. 39–42). London: Falmer Press.

Firestone, W.A. and Corbett, H.D. (1988) Planned organizational change. In Boyan, N.J. (ed.), *Handbook of Research on Educational Administration* (pp. 321–40). New York: Longman.

Fontana, A. and Frey, J.H. (2000) The interview: from structured questions to negotiated text. In Denzin, N.K. and Lincoln, Y.S. (eds), *Handbook of Qualitative Research* (2nd edn) (pp. 645–72). Thousand Oaks, CA: Sage.

Ford, J., Hughes, M., and Ruebain, D. (1999) *Education Law and Practice.* London: Legal Action Group.

Foskett, N. (2003) Market, policies, management and leadership in school. In Davies, B. and West-Burnham, J. (eds), *Handbook of Educational Leadership and Management* (pp. 177–86). London: Pearson.

Friedman, I. (2003) School organizational values: the driving force for effectiveness and change. In Begley, P.T. and Johansson, O. (eds), *The Ethical Dimensions of School Leadership* (pp. 162–79). Dordrecht: Kluwer.

Fullan, M. (1991) *The New Meaning of Educational Change*. London: Cassell.

—— (2003) *The Moral Imperative of School Leadership*. Thousand Oaks, CA: Corwin Press.

Fuller, L.L. (1977) Some presuppositions shaping the concept of socialization. In Tapp, J.L. and Levine, F.J. (eds), *Law, Justice and the Individual in Society.* New York: Holt, Rinehart & Winston.

Gewirtz, S. (1998) Post-welfarist schooling: a social justice audit. *Education and Social Justice*, 1 (1): 52–63.

Gibton, D. (2000) Training principal-candidates as moral, political and communal leaders: scruffy is successful. Paper presented at the annual meeting of the American Educational Research Association, New Orleans, April.

—— (2001) 'Once the government provided education. Now it provides information on education': insights from what UK headteachers think of educational law regarding decentralization policy, self-management and autonomy. Paper presented at the annual conference of the British Educational Leadership, Management, and Administration Society (BELMAS), Newport Pagnell, UK, October.

—— (2003) Educational leadership and the tensions and dilemmas of decentralization and centralization. In Davies, B. and West-Burnham, J. (eds), *Handbook of Educational Leadership and Management* (pp. 671–83). London: Pearson.

—— (2004) Minding the gap: principals' graphic mindscapes on educational policy and law-based reform: a technique for second degree qualitative policy analysis. *Studies in Educational Evaluation,* (forthcoming).

—— and Goldring, E. (2002) The role of legislation in educational decentralization: the case of Israel and the United Kingdom. *Peabody Journal of Education*, 76 (3, 40): 81–101.

—— Goldring, E.B., and Sabar, N. (1998) A comparative and empirical view of decentralization policy, legislation and autonomy in Israel's school system: an unattainable aspiration. Paper presented at the annual meeting of the American Educational Research Association, San Diego, April.

—— Sabar, N., and Goldring, E.B. (2000) How principals of autonomous schools in Israel view implementation of decentralization and restructuring policy: risks, rights and wrongs. *Educational Evaluation and Policy Analysis*, 22 (2): 193–210.

Giddens, A. (1998) *The Third Way*. Cambridge, UK: Polity Press.

Gillborn, D. (1998) Racism, selection, poverty, and parents: New Labour – old problems? *Journal of Educational Policy*, 13 (6): 17–35.

—— and Youdell, D. (2000) *Rationing Education: Policy, Practice, Reform and Equity*. Buckingham, UK: Open University Press.

Ginsberg, M. and Berry, B. (1998) The capability for enhancing accountability. In Macpherson, R.J.S. (ed.), *The Politics of Accountability: Educative and International Perspectives* (pp. 43–61). Thousand Oaks, CA: Corwin Press.

Giroux, H.A. (1992) Educational leadership and the crisis of democratic government. *Educational Researcher*, 21 (4): 4–11.

Glatter, R. (2002) Governance, autonomy and accountability in education. In Bush, T. and Bell, L. (eds), *The Principles and Practice of Educational Management* (pp. 225–40). London: Paul Chapman/Sage.

—— (2003) Governance and educational innovation. In Davies, B. and West-Burnham, J. (eds), *Handbook of Educational Leadership and Management* (pp. 228–37). London: Pearson.

Goertz, M.E. (1999) The finance of American public education: challenges of equity, adequacy and efficiency. In Cizek, G.J. (ed.), *Handbook of Educational Policy* (pp. 32–53). San Diego: Academic Press.

Gold, A. and Evans, J. (2002) Piggy in the middle: middle managers, emergent leaders or prospective senior leaders? Paper presented at the annual conference of the British Educational Leadership, Management, and Administration Society (BELMAS), Birmingham, UK, September.

Gold, R. and Szemerenyi, S. (1999) *Running a School 2000/2001: Legal Duties and Responsibilities*. Bristol, UK: Jordans.

Goldring, E. and Greenfield, W. (2002) Understanding the evolving concept of leadership in education: roles, expectations and dilemmas. In Murphy, J. (ed.), *The Educational Leadership Challenge: Redefining Leadership for the 21st Century* (pp. 1–19). Chicago: NSSE/University of Chicago Press.

—— and Rallis, S.F. (1993) *Principals of Dynamic Schools: Taking Charge of Change*. Newbury Park, CA: Corwin-Sage.

—— Crowson, R., Laird, D., and Berk, R. (2002) Unmaking desegregation policy and 'going unitary': the loss of a sense of place. Paper presented at the annual meeting of the American Educational Research Association, New Orleans, April.

Gray, J. and Reynolds D. (1996) The challenges of school improvement: preparing for the long haul. In Gray, J., Reynolds D., Fitz-Gibbon, C., and Jesson, D. (eds), *Merging Traditions: The Future of Research on School Effectiveness and School Improvement*. London: Cassell.

Hallinger, P. and Hausman, C. (1994) From Attila the Hun to Mary had a Little Lamb: principals' role ambiguity in restructured schools. In Murphy, J. and

Seashore-Louis, K. (eds), *Reshaping the Principalship: Insights from Transformational Reform Efforts* (pp. 154–76). Thousand Oaks, CA: Corwin Press.

Hammersley, M. (ed.) (2002) *Educational Research: Policymaking and Practice.* London: Paul Chapman/Sage.

—— and Gomm, R. (2002) Research and practice, two worlds for ever at odds? In Hammersley, M. (ed.), *Educational Research: Policymaking and Practice* (pp. 59–82). London: Paul Chapman/Sage.

Hannaway, J. (1993) Decentralization in two school districts: challenging the standard paradigm. In Hannaway, J. and Carnoy, M. (eds), *Decentralization and School Improvement* (pp. 135–62). San Francisco: Jossey-Bass.

—— (2004) Accountability, assessment, and performance issues: we've come a long way – or have we? In Boyd, W.L. and Miretzky, D. (eds), *American Educational Governance on Trial: Change and Challenges – the 102nd Yearbook of the National Society for the Study of Education (NSSE)* (pp. 20–36). Chicago: Chicago University Press.

Hargreaves, A. (1995) *Changing Teachers, Changing Times: Teachers' Work and Culture in the Postmodern Age.* London: Cassell.

—— and Fink, D. (2003) Sustaining leadership. In Davies, B. and West-Burnham, J. (eds), *Handbook of Educational Leadership and Management* (pp. 435–50). London: Pearson.

—— and Fullan, M. (1998) *What's Worth Fighting for in Education?* Buckingham, UK: Open University Press.

Harris, A. (2001) Building the capacity for school improvement. *School Leadership and Management,* 21 (30): 261–70.

—— (2004) Distributed leadership and school improvement. *Educational Management, Administration and Leadership,* 32 (1): 11–24.

Harris, N. (1993) *Law and Education: Regulation, Consumerism and the Education System.* London: Sweet & Maxwell.

—— (1996) *The Law Relating to Schools* (2nd edn). London: Sweet & Maxwell.

—— (1999) Too bad? The closure of Hackney Downs School under Section 225 of the Education Act 1993. *Education and the Law,* 8 (2): 109–25.

—— (2000) Education law: excluding the child. *Education and the Law,* 21 (1): 31–46.

Hentchke, G. and Davies, B. (1997) Rethinking the educational context: a re-engineering approach. In Davies, B. and Ellison, L. (eds), *School Leadership for the 21st Century: A Competency and Knowledge Approach* (pp. 23–35). London: Routledge.

Heubert, J.R. (1997) Schools without rules? Charter schools, federal disability law, and the paradoxes of deregulation. *Harvard Civil Rights – Civil Liberties Law Review,* 32 (2): 301–53.

—— (ed.) (1999a) *Law and School Reform: Six Strategies for Promoting Educational Equity*. New Haven: Yale University Press.

—— (1999b) Six law-driven reforms: developments, lessons, and prospects. In Heubert, J.R. (ed.), *Law and School Reform: Six Strategies for Promoting Educational Equity* (pp. 1–38). New Haven: Yale University Press.

Hill, P.T. (2004) What's wrong with public education governance in big cities and how should it be fixed? In Boyd, W.L. and Miretzky, D. (eds), *American Educational Governance on Trial: Change and Challenges – the 102nd Yearbook of the National Society for the Study of Education (NSSE)* (pp. 57–81). Chicago: Chicago University Press.

House, E.R. (1996) A framework for appraising educational reforms. *Educational Researcher*, 25 (7): 6–14.

Hutchinson, S. (1988) Grounded theory. In Sherman, R.R. and Webb, R.B. (eds), *Qualitative Research in Education: Focus and Methods* (pp. 123–40). London: Falmer Press.

Hyams, O. (1997) What does it mean to be *in loco parentis*? *Education and the Law*, 9 (3): 187–94.

Jackson, B.S. (1985) *Semiotics and Legal Theory*. London: Routledge, Kegan & Paul.

James, C. (2003) The work of educational leaders in building creative and passionate schools and colleges. Paper presented at the annual conference of the British Educational Leadership, Management, and Administration Society (BELMAS), Kent Hill, UK, October.

Jefferson, A.L. (1996) The Alberta case: the challenge to the School Amendment Act, 1994 and Provincial Achievements of Fiscal Equity. *Journal of Educational Administration and Foundations*, 11 (2): 56–79.

Johnson, H. (2003) The role of the headteacher in promoting national identity: a bilingual faith school case study. Paper presented at the annual conference of the British Educational Leadership, Management, and Administration Society (BELMAS), Kent Hill, UK, October.

Kaye, T. (1998) Admissions to school: efficiency versus parental choice? *Education and the Law*, 10 (1): 19–33.

—— (2001) *Education Law and Practice*. London: Blackstone.

Kennedy, M. (1999) Infusing educational decision making with research. In Cizek, G.J. (ed.), *Handbook of Educational Policy* (pp. 54–81). San Diego: Academic Press.

Kirst, M. (2004) Mayoral influence, new regimes, and public school governance. In Boyd, W.L. and Miretzky, D. (eds), *American Educational Governance on Trial: Change and Challenges – the 102nd Yearbook of the National Society for the Study of Education (NSSE)* (pp. 196–218). Chicago: Chicago University Press.

Koehn, D. (1994) *The Ground of Professional Ethics*. London: Routledge.

LaMorte, M. (2002) *School Law: Cases and Concepts* (7th edn). Boston: Allyn & Bacon.

Leithwood, K. and Aitken, R. (1995) *Making Schools Smarter: A System for Monitoring School and District Progress*. Thousand Oaks, CA: Corwin Press.

—— Jantzi, D., and Steinbach, R. (1999) *Changing Leadership for Changing Times*. Buckingham, UK: Open University Press.

—— and Steinbach, R. (2003) Successful leadership for especially challenging schools. In Davies, B. and West-Burnham, J. (eds), *Handbook of Educational Leadership and Management* (pp. 25–43). London: Pearson.

Levacic, R. (1995) *Local Management of Schools: Analysis and Practice*. Buckingham, UK: Open University Press.

—— (2002) Efficiency, equity and autonomy. In Bush, T. and Bell, L. (eds), *The Principles and Practice of Educational Management* (pp. 187–206). London: Paul Chapman/Sage.

—— Simmons, K., and Smales, L. (2003) The missing bucks: Buckinghamshire upper schools forum campaign for fair funding and the use of research evidence. Paper presented at the annual conference of the British Educational Leadership, Management, and Administration Society (BELMAS), Kent Hill, UK, October.

—— and Woods, P.A. (2000) The impact of quasi-markets and performance regulation on socially disadvantaged schools. Paper presented at the annual meeting of the American Educational Research Association, New Orleans, April.

Levin, H.M. (1990) Why isn't educational research more useful? In Anderson, D.S. and Biddle, B.J. (eds), *Knowledge for Policy: Improving Education through Policy* (pp. 70–8). London: Falmer Press.

Lewis, A.C. (1999) Educational policy analysis: the trends behind, the trends ahead. In Cizek, G.J. (ed.), *Handbook of Educational Policy* (pp. 523–30). San Diego: Academic Press.

Lewis, D.A. (1993) Deinstitutionalization and school decentralization: making the same mistake twice. In Hannaway, J. and Carnoy, M. (eds), *Decentralization and School Improvement* (pp. 84–101). San Francisco: Jossey-Bass.

Lincoln, Y.S. and Denzin, N.K. (2000) The seventh moment: out of the past. In Denzin, N.K. and Lincoln, Y.S. (eds), *Handbook of Qualitative Research* (2nd edn) (pp. 1047–65). Thousand Oaks, CA: Sage.

—— and Guba, E.G. (2000) Paradigmatic controversies, contradictions, and emerging confluences. In Denzin, N.K. and Lincoln, Y.S. (eds), *Handbook of Qualitative Research* (2nd edn) (pp. 163–88). Thousand Oaks, CA: Sage.

Linn, R.L. (2003) Accountability: responsibility and reasonable expectations. *Educational Researcher*, 32 (7): 3–13.

Lubienski, C. (2002) The politics of 'The Public' in public education. Paper presented at the annual meeting of the American Educational Research Association, New Orleans, April.

MacDonald, B. (1991) Critical introduction: from innovation to reform – a framework for analysing change. In Rudduck, J. (ed.), *Innovation and Change* (pp. 1–13). Buckingham, UK: Open University Press.

McDonnell, L. (1989) *Restructuring American Schools*. New York: National Center on Education and Employment.

McGaughy, C.L. (2000) The role of education in community development: the Akron enterprise community initiative. Paper presented at the annual meeting of the American Educational Research Association, New Orleans, April.

McLaughlin, M. and Shepard, L. (1995) *Improving Education through Standards-Based Reform: A Report of the National Academy of Education Panel on Standards-Based Reform*. Stanford, CA: The National Academy of Education.

McUsic, M.S. (1999) The law's role in the distribution of education: the promises and pitfalls of school finance litigation. In Heubert, J.R. (ed.), *Law and School Reform: Six Strategies for Promoting Educational Equity* (pp. 88–159). New Haven: Yale University Press.

Maykut, P. and Morehouse, R. (1994) *Beginning Qualitative Research: A Philosophic and Practical Guide*. London: Falmer Press.

Mehan, H., Datnow, A., and Hubbard, L. (2003) Why educational reforms sustain or fail: lessons for educational leaders. In Davies, B. and West-Burnham, J. (eds), *Handbook of Educational Leadership and Management* (pp. 460–77). London: Pearson.

Meredith, P. (2000) The contracting out of LEA functions and implications for democracy and accountability. *Education and the Law*, 12 (1): 5–9.

Meyer, J.W. and Scott, W.R. (1983) *Organizational Environments: Ritual and Rationality*. Beverly Hills, CA: Sage.

Miles, M. and Huberman, M. (1994) *Qualitative Data Analysis: An Expanded Sourcebook* (2nd edn). Beverly Hills, CA: Sage.

Mill, J.S. (1977) *On Liberty*. In *The Collected Works of J.S. Mill*, vol. 28, Toronto: University of Toronto Press.

Milstein, M.M. (1990) Rethinking the clinical aspect of preparation programs: from theory to practice. In Jacobson, S.L. and Conway, J.A. (eds), *Educational Leadership in an Age of Reform* (pp. 119–30). New York: Longman.

Minow, M. (1993) Law and social change. *UMKC Law Review*, 62 (1): 171–83.

Miron, G. and Nelson, C. (2002) *What's Public about Charter Schools? Lessons Learned about Choice and Accountability*. Thousand Oaks, CA: Corwin Press.

Mitchell, D.E. and Encarnation, D.J. (1984) Alternative state policy mechanisms for influencing school performance. *Educational Researcher*, 13 (5): 4–11.

Monk, D. (1997) School exclusions and the 1997 Education Act. *Education and the Law*, 9 (4): 277–90.

Morrison, K. (2002) *School Leadership and Complexity Theory*. London: Routledge/ Falmer.

Murphy, J. (1992) *The Landscape of Leadership Preparation: Reframing the Education of School Administrators*. Newbury Park, CA: Corwin Press.

—— (1993) Restructuring schooling: the equity infrastructure. *School Effectiveness and School Improvement*, 4 (2): 111–30.

—— (1994) Transformed change and the evolving role of the principal: early empirical evidence. In Murphy, J. and Seashore-Louis, K. (eds), *Reshaping the Principalship: Insights from Transformational Reform Efforts* (pp. 20–56). Thousand Oaks, CA: Corwin Press.

—— (2002) Reculturing the profession of educational leadership. In Murphy, J. (ed.), *The Educational Leadership Challenge: Redefining Leadership for the 21st Century* (pp. 65–82). Chicago: NSSE/University of Chicago Press.

—— and Beck, L.G. (1994) Reconstructing the principalship: challenges and possibilities. In Murphy, J. and Seashore-Louis, K. (eds), *Reshaping the Principalship: Insights from Transformational Reform Efforts* (pp. 3–19). Thousand Oaks, CA: Corwin Press.

Muth, R. and Segall, R. (1993) Toward restructuring: developing cooperative practices in schools. Paper presented at the annual meeting of the American Educational Research Association, Atlanta.

NCSL (2003) *National Standards for Headteachers: Draft Consultation Document on Proposals for Revised Standards* (September). Nottingham: National College for School Leadership. (http://www.ncsl.org.uk/index.cfm?pageid=national-standards-headteachers)

Nevo, D. (1995) *School-based Evaluation: A Dialogue For School Improvement*. Oxford, UK: Pergamon Press.

Odden, A. (1991) The evolution of educational policy implementation. In Odden, A.R. (ed.), *Educational Policy Implementation* (pp. 1–13). Albany: State University of New York.

Ogawa, R. and Bossert, S.T. (2000) Leadership as an organizational quality. In *The Jossey-Bass Reader on Educational Leadership* (pp. 38–58). San Francisco: Jossey-Bass.

—— Crowson, R., and Goldring, E.B. (1999) Enduring dilemmas of school organization. In Murphy, J. and Seashore-Louis, K. (eds), *Handbook of Research on Educational Administration* (pp. 277–95). San Francisco: Jossey-Bass.

Orfield, G. (1999) Conservative activists and the rush toward resegregation. In Heubert, J.R. (ed.), *Law and School Reform: Six Strategies for Promoting Educational Equity* (pp. 39–87). New Haven: Yale University Press.

Ouston, J. and Davies, J. (1998) OFSTED and afterwards? Schools' responses to inspection. In Earley, P. (ed.), *School Improvement After Inspection: School and LEA Responses* (pp. 13–24). London: Paul Chapman/Sage.

—— Fidler, B., and Earley, P. (1998) The educational accountability of schools in England and Wales. In Macpherson, R.J.S. (ed.), *The Politics of Accountability: Educative and International Perspectives* (pp. 107–19). Thousand Oaks, CA: Corwin Press.

Parker-Jenkins, M. (1998) Equality before the law: an exploration of the pursuit of government funding by Muslim schools in Britain. Paper presented at the annual meeting of the American Educational Research Association, San Diego, April.

Parry, G. and Parry, A.M. (2000) Implications of the Human Rights Act (1998) for schools. *Education and the Law*, 12 (4): 279–85.

Patton, M.Q. (1980) *Qualitative Evaluation*. Beverly Hills, CA: Sage.

Popkewitz, T.S. (1999a) Critical traditions, modernisms, and the 'posts'. In Popkewitz, T.S. and Fender, L. (eds), *Critical Theories in Education: Changing Terrains of Knowledge and Politics* (pp. 1–16). New York: Routledge.

—— (1999b) A social epistemology of educational research. In Popkewitz, T.S. and Fender, L. (eds), *Critical Theories in Education: Changing Terrains of Knowledge and Politics* (pp. 17–44). New York: Routledge.

Prestine, N.A. (2000) Enabler or restrainer? Factors that determine administrator response to systemic change initiatives. Paper presented at the annual meeting of the American Educational Research Association, New Orleans, April.

Pullin, D. (1999) Whose schools are these and what are they for? The role of the rule of law in defining educational opportunity in American public education. In Cizek, G.J. (ed.), *Handbook of Educational Policy* (pp. 4–31). San Diego: Academic Press.

Radnor, H.A., Ball, S.J., and Vincent, C. (1998) Local educational governance: accountability and democracy in the United Kingdom. In Macpherson, R.J.S. (ed.), *The Politics of Accountability: Educative and International Perspectives* (pp. 120–33). Thousand Oaks, CA: Corwin Press.

Rawls, J. (1971) *A Theory of Justice*. Cambridge, MA: Belknap-Harvard University Press.

Reglin, G.L. (1992) Public school educators' knowledge of selected Supreme Court decisions affecting daily public school operations. *Journal of Educational Administration*, 30 (2): 26–31.

Riehl, C.J. (2000) The principal's role in creating inclusive schools for diverse students: a review of normative, empirical, and critical literature on the practice of educational administration. *Review of Educational Research*, 70 (1): 55–81.

Rousseau, J.J. (1978) *The Social Contract* (ed. Masters, R.D.). New York: St Martins.

Ruff, A. (1999) Admissions appeals in 1999: the impact of the 1998 regulations and R. *v.* Birmingham City Council *ex parte*. *Education and the Law*, 11 (4): 77–87.

—— (2002) *Education Law: Texts, Cases and Materials* (pp. 153–260). London: Butterworths.

Sarason, S.B. (1982) *The Culture of the School and the Problem of Change* (2nd edn). Boston: Allyn & Bacon.

Schiff, D.N. (1981) Law as a social phenomenon. In Podgorecki, A. and Whelan, C.J. (eds), *Sociological Approaches to Law* (pp. 151–66). London: Croom Helm.

Schon, D.A. (1983) *The Reflective Practitioner: How Professionals Think in Action*. New York: Basic Books.

Seashore-Louis, K. and Murphy, J. (1994) The evolving role of the principal: some concluding thoughts. In Murphy, J. and Seashore-Louis, K. (eds), *Reshaping the Principalship: Insights from Transformational Reform Efforts* (pp. 265–81). Thousand Oaks, CA: Corwin Press.

Sergiovanni, T.J. (1994) *Building Community in Schools*. San Francisco: Jossey-Bass.

—— (1995) *The Principalship: A Reflective Practice Perspective*. Boston, MA: Allyn & Bacon.

—— (2002) *Leadership: What's in it for Schools?* Thousand Oaks, CA: Corwin Press.

Slavin, R.E. (1999a) Success for all: policy consequences of replicable schoolwide reform. In Cizek, G.J. (ed.), *Handbook of Educational Policy* (pp. 326–50). San Diego: Academic Press.

—— (1999b) The pendulum revisited: faddism in education and its alternatives. In Cizek, G.J. (ed.), *Handbook of Educational Policy* (pp. 375–86). San Diego: Academic Press.

Smith, S.C. and Piele, P.K. (1997) *School Leadership: Handbook for Excellence*. Eugene, OR: ERIC.

Smrekar, C. (1996) *The Impact of School Choice and Community: In the Interest of Families and Schools*. Albany: State University of New York Press.

Stake, R.E. (1997) Case study methods in educational research: seeking sweet water. In Jaeger, R.M. (ed.), *Complementary Methods for Research in Education* (2nd edn) (pp. 401–14). Washington, DC: American Educational Research Association.

Starr, T.R. (1982) *The Social Transformation of American Medicine*. New York: Basic Books.

Stoll, L. and Earl, L. (2003) Making it last: building capacity for sustainability. In Davies, B. and West-Burnham, J. (eds), *Handbook of Educational Leadership and Management* (pp. 491–504). London: Pearson.

Strauss, A.L. (1987) *Qualitative Analysis for Social Scientists*. Cambridge: Cambridge University Press.

—— and Corbin, J. (1994) Grounded theory methodology: an overview. In Denzin, N.K. and Lincoln, Y.S. (eds) *Handbook of Qualitative Research* (pp. 273–85). Thousand Oaks, CA: Sage.

Strike, K.A. (2004) Liberty, democracy, and community: legitimacy in public education. In Boyd, W.L. and Miretzky, D. (eds), *American Educational Governance on Trial: Change and Challenges – the 102nd Yearbook of the National Society for the Study of Education (NSSE)* (pp. 37–56). Chicago: Chicago University Press.

Talbot, D.L. and Crow, G.M. (1998) When school changed, did I get a new job? Principals' role conceptions in a restructuring context. Paper presented at the annual meeting of the American Educational Research Association, San Diego, April.

Thornton, C. and Wongbundhit, Y. (2002) An evolution from Miami-Dade USI to Miami RISE-USP. Paper presented at the annual meeting of the American Educational Research Association, New Orleans, April.

Tooley, J. (1996) Loopholes in the National Curriculum? The genesis and use of Sections 16 and 17 of the 1988 Education Reform Act. *Education and the Law*, 8 (4): 319–30.

Torres, C.A. (1999) Critical theory and political sociology of education. In Popkewitz, T.S. and Fender, L. (eds), *Critical Theories in Education: Changing Terrains of Knowledge and Politics* (pp. 87–116). New York: Routledge.

Tyack, D.B. and Cuban, L. (1995) *Tinkering Toward Utopia*. Cambridge, MA: Harvard University Press.

—— James, T., and Benavot, A. (1987) *Law and the Shaping of Public Education, 1785–1954*. Madison: University of Wisconsin Press.

Vidich, A.J. and Lyman, S.M. (2000) Qualitative methods: their history in sociology and anthropology. In Denzin, N.K. and Lincoln, Y.S. (eds), *Handbook of Qualitative Research* (2nd edn) (pp. 37–84). Thousand Oaks, CA: Sage.

Vogel, L.R., Rau, W.C., Ashby, D., and Baker, P. (2002) A decade of turbulence: the voice of principals caught in the middle of Illinois school reform. Paper presented at the annual meeting of the American Educational Research Association, New Orleans, April.

Volansky, A. (2003) *The Pendulum Syndrome Centralisation and Decentralisation in England and Wales*. Tel-Aviv: Ramot Publications, Tel-Aviv University.

Walford, G. (1990) School choice and the quasi-market. In Walford, G. (ed.), *Privatization and Privilege in Education* (pp. 7–15). London: Routledge.

Wayne-MacKay, A. and Sutherland, L. (1990) Canada. In Birch, I.K. and Richter, I. (eds), *Comparative School Law* (pp. 170–254). Oxford: Pergamon Press.

Weckstein, P. (1999) School reform and enforceable rights to quality education. In Heubert, J.R. (ed.), *Law and School Reform: Six Strategies for Promoting Educational Equity* (pp. 306–93). New Haven: Yale University Press.

Weiler, H.N. (1993) Control versus legitimization: the politics of ambivalence. In Hannaway, J. and Carnoy, M. (eds), *Decentralization and School Improvement* (pp. 55–83). San Francisco: Jossey-Bass.

Weindling, D. and Earley, P. (1987) *Secondary Headship: The First Years*. Windsor, UK: NFER-Nelson.

Welner, K. (2000) Reclaiming a refuge: can equity-minded education policies once again be promoted through the judiciary? Paper presented at the annual meeting of the American Educational Research Association, New Orleans, April.

Whitaker, P. (1997) Changes in professional development: the personal dimension. In Kydd, L., Crawford, M., and Riches, C. (eds) *Professional Development for Educational Management* (pp. 11–25). Buckingham, UK: Open University Press.

Whitty, G., Power, S., and Halpin, D. (1998) *Devolution and Choice in Education: The School, the State and the Market*. Buckingham, UK: Open University Press.

Wildy, H. and Louden, W. (2000) School restructuring and the dilemmas of principals' work. *Educational Management and Administration*, 28 (2): 173–84.

Wong, K.K. (1999) Political institutions and educational policy. In Cizek, G.J. (ed.), *Handbook of Educational Policy* (pp. 297–324). San Diego: Academic Press.

—— and Anagnostopoulos, D. (1998) Can integrated governance reconstruct teaching? Lessons learned from two low-performing Chicago high-schools. In Macpherson, R.J.S. (ed.), *The Politics of Accountability: Educative and International Perspectives* (pp. 26 42). Thousand Oaks, CA: Corwin Press.

Woods, P.A. (2000) Varieties and themes in producer engagement: structure and agency in the schools public-market. *British Journal of Sociology of Education*, 21 (2): 219–42.

—— Jeffrey, B., Troman, G., and Boyle, M. (1997) *Restructuring Schools, Reconstructing Teachers: Responding to Change in the Primary School*. Buckingham, UK: Open University Press.

Wright, N. (2002) Between a rock and a hard place: heads of department in New Zealand secondary schools. Paper presented at the annual conference of the British Educational Leadership, Management, and Administration Society (BELMAS), Birmingham, UK, September.

Zelman, C.C. and Bryant, M.T. (2002) The Solomonic pathway: critical incidents in the elementary school principalship. Paper presented at the annual meeting of the American Educational Research Association, New Orleans, April.

Subject index

Name index